PATCHWORK

PATCHWORK

Hilary More
Series Editor: Rosemary Wilkinson

SELECT EDITIONS

Note: Imperial and metric measurements are not direct equivalents, so always follow only one set in a particular method.

The edition first published in 1994 by
Promotional Reprint Company Ltd., Deacon House, 65 Old Church Street,
London SW3 5BS

Created and produced by
Rosemary Wilkinson and Malcolm Saunders Publishing Ltd
4 Lonsdale Square, London N1 1EN

ISBN 1 85648 275 8

Printed and bound in Hong Kong

Illustrations: Kate Simunck
Design: Ming Cheung
Cover photograph: Empress Mills (1927) Ltd, Empress Street, Colne,
Lancashire BB8 9HU

Contents

Introduction

Patchwork is an ingenious way of recycling fabric remnants. Its origins can be found way back in history when economy was the reason behind the craft: old or worn furnishings and clothes were cut into patches and rejoined to make warm quilts and other furnishings for the home. The more controlled pieced work we recognise today became commonplace during the seventeenth and eighteenth centuries.

Patchwork skills were taken by the New World settlers from England to America, where the pioneer women developed their own style. As the craft spread, groups of stitchers worked together creating specific patterns and designs. While patchwork waned in popularity in England, it flourished in the United States. The circle was eventually completed when the American style of patchwork returned to England where it has been re-adopted with great enthusiasm.

There is, therefore, a natural division of styles between American patchwork, which is generally machine-stitched together in geometrical blocks, and English patchwork, which is composed of small regular patches, such as hexagons, and is usually worked by hand.

Part 1:
EQUIPMENT

Fabric

Patchwork pieces can be cut from any material, but natural fabrics work best. To create accurate patches the fabrics need to fold into sharp creases and be easy to sew. The ideal fabric is a firm closely-woven, opaque cotton fabric, pre-shrunk and colourfast. As well as pure cotton, fine linens and wools and some silks are also suitable. Leather can also make a good patchwork fabric. Try to avoid man-made fabrics which can be hard to cut out accurately and too slippery to stitch neatly.

Points to remember when choosing fabric for patchwork:

⋆ All the fabric in one piece of work should be of the same weight so the patches lie flat when joined together.

⋆ The patches should be able to be laundered together, so place cottons with cottons, all silks together, etc.

⋆ Wash all the fabric before cutting out the patches, to check for colour fastness and shrinkage, then press well to remove all creases.

⋆ Check that the fabric is not so fine that the turnings can be seen on the right side. If you need to use fine fabrics, back the patches with a layer of iron-on interfacing.

⋆ Velvet and fine cords can be used provided you allow for the direction of the pile. This can also be used to good advantage as part of the design.

⋆ When recycling fabric from a garment, first unpick all the seams and wash and press the fabric. Then trim off all the seam allowances and any worn sections.

⋆ If you are keen to use a variety of fabric types

from your scrap bag, then choose "Crazy patchwork" (see page 47) to make a quilt or cover, for which mixing an odd assortment of fabrics together creates a fun result.

Lining fabrics

Pick a fabric that is compatible in weight and construction to the patchwork pieces. Check that the lining can also be laundered in the same way, so the whole quilt or cover can be quickly and easily cleaned. When deciding on colour, look at the whole patchwork and aim for one that will tone in with all the fabrics without being too distracting.

Needles

Needles for hand stitching come in a huge range of types and sizes and as with general sewing, for patchwork it is important to match the needle to the job.

⋆ Use Sharps in sizes 9 or 10 for tacking the fabric allowances around the paper linings.

⋆ Choose Betweens in sizes 9 or 10 for hand sewing the patchwork pieces together. These needles are short and sharp and perfect for fine stitching. Remember, the higher the number the finer the needle.

⋆ Crewel needles are sharp medium-length needles used for embroidery, but they can also be used for patchwork, provided they are fine.

Match sewing machine needles to the fabric - check the machine instruction booklet for guidelines, and make sure that the needle is sharp.

Pins

Choose fine brass lace pins, which do not rust, so they will not mark the fabric when holding the paper linings in place or when pinning patches together ready for stitching.

Threads

Tack the paper linings in position or the fabric patches together with a soft tacking thread. This loosely-twisted cotton thread can be quickly removed from the fabric after the main stitching is complete.

Match the main sewing thread to the fabric, using fine cotton thread with cotton fabrics and silk thread with silks and velvets. Pick a neutral colour that can be used to stitch all the fabric patches together for the whole project.

Beeswax

Beeswax is not an essential part of the workbox but if when hand stitching, you run the working thread through beeswax it will strengthen the thread as well as making it easier to use.

Thimble

A thimble will help to push the needle through the fabric when hand stitching patchwork. Pick one that sits comfortably on the middle finger of the right (left) hand.

Cutting equipment

You will need three pairs of scissors for patchwork: a sharp pair of dressmakers' shears for cutting out fabric; a separate pair of sharp scissors for cutting out the paper linings and a small pair of sewing scissors for snipping threads and into seam allowances.

Alternatively, a rotary cutter can be used. This sharp cutting wheel is ideal for patchwork. Used together with a special mat, this cutter will save time as several layers of fabric can be cut together.

Use a sharp craft knife and a metal ruler for cutting card templates.

Tape measure

Always keep a tape measure handy for measuring fabric amounts and seam allowances.

Quilter's handle

This handle holds the marking tools firmly in place while marking and cutting. It lifts straight off the fabric, preventing distortion.

Quilter's rule

Clear plastic ruler with marked horizontal and vertical grid lines to help make marking more accurate. They come in a variety of lengths and widths.

Quilter's triangle

Made of clear plastic, this right-angle triangle will

help to obtain straight right-angle edges when marking and cutting out fabric patches.

Dream seamer/Seam wheel

This looks like a small coin with a central hole. Fit a pencil point in the hole and run the wheel alongside the edges of a curved or straight-edge template and you will mark an even 1/4in (5mm) seam allowance with ease.

Marking equipment

There are different methods of marking patchwork shapes onto fabric. Tailors' chalk comes in a range of colours which show up well on cotton fabric. Water-erasible marking pens are a useful alternative to chalk. Test first on a spare piece of fabric as the marking lines may be hard to conceal or remove. A soft pencil can be used to mark on the wrong side of the fabrics. A sharp, hard pencil is needed for marking out templates and paper linings.

Drafting equipment

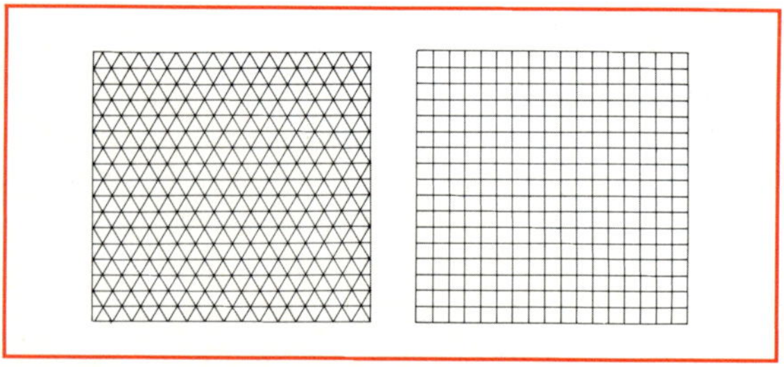

Left: isometric; right: squared graph paper

For charting patchwork designs you will need a range of pencils and crayons as well as squared and isometric graph paper.

A pair of compasses will help with drawing circles and a protractor for dividing up circles and creating pentagon templates, plus a ruler for straight lines.

Templates

Templates are the patterns used for cutting the paper linings and fabric shapes. Shop-bought templates are made in plastic or metal and are available in a variety of shapes and sizes.

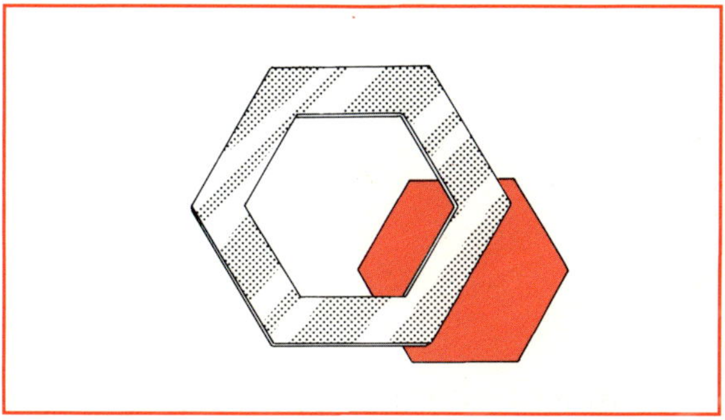

Template pairs

Templates also come in pairs, a small metal template combined with a larger transparent plastic window template. The metal template is the finished size of the patch and is used to cut the paper linings. The window template is ¼in (5mm) larger all around and used to cut the fabric. The ¼in (5mm) allowance folds over the lining to form the patch. The clear window makes it possible to position a motif centrally on a fabric patch (see page 27).

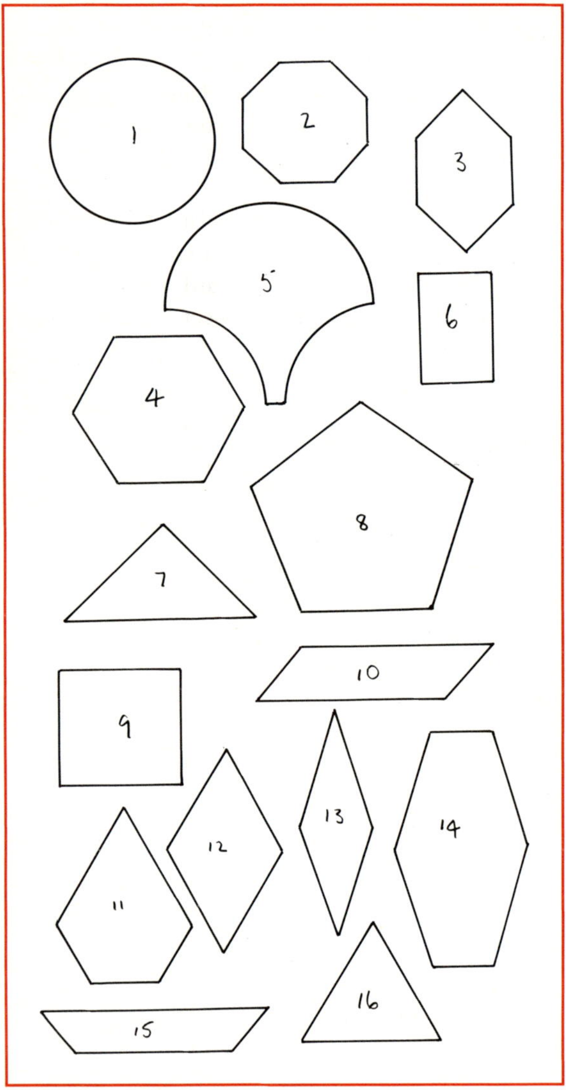

Template shapes (see key opposite)

The most popular templates are the square, hexagon (honeycomb), triangle, diamond, long hexagon (church window), octagon and clamshell. These and other less common shapes are shown in the illustration opposite.

You can also cut your own templates from stiff card or template plastic, but they must be accurate for a perfect result (see page 18). As card does not last long, when stitching a large project cut out more than one template.

key to templates

1 circle
2 octagon
3 long hexagon (church window)
4 hexagon
5 clamshell
6 rectangle
7 isosceles triangle
8 pentagon
9 square
10 parallelogram
11 irregular pentagon
12 short diamond
13 long diamond
14 coffin
15 trapezoid
16 equilateral triangle

Paper Linings

Use a template to mark and cut the paper linings from the stiff pages of magazines, old greetings cards or cartridge paper. Freezer paper is particularly useful as it is slightly adhesive when ironed onto the fabric template.

Iron

A good steam and dry iron is a must for patchwork stitchers. You can press the patches to create a firm outline and the seams as they are stitched either open or to one side.

Part 2:
TECHNIQUES

How to Construct a Template

Squares and rectangles

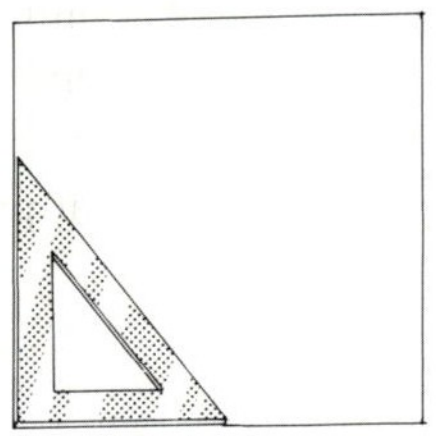

Creating a square

Squares and rectangles are easy to construct. Use a good ruler and a set square to make sure that all the sides are straight and at right angles to the other sides. Cut with a rotary cutter or sharp craft knife and metal ruler.

Hexagons

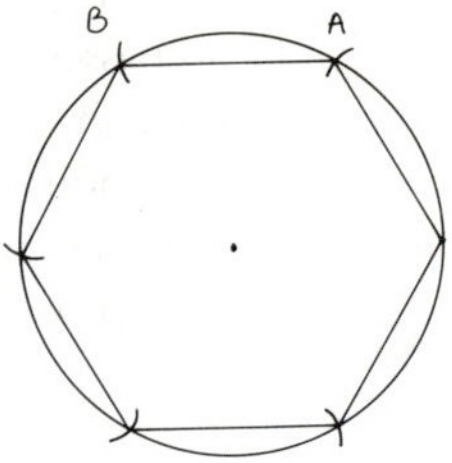

Constructing a hexagon

Decide on the finished size of the hexagon from point to point and set a pair of compasses to the radius of a circle of this size. Draw a circle outline on template card or plastic. With the compasses still set at this measurement, place the point anywhere on the circle and draw an arc where the pencil crosses the outline (point A on the diagram). Place the point of the compasses at point A and draw another arc across the circle outline (point B). Repeat all around the circle. Using a ruler and pencil, join up the six equidistant points to form the hexagon.

Long diamonds

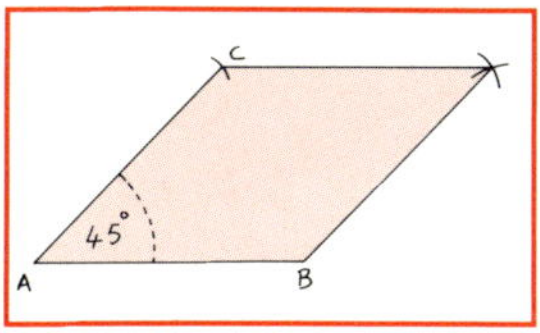

Long diamond

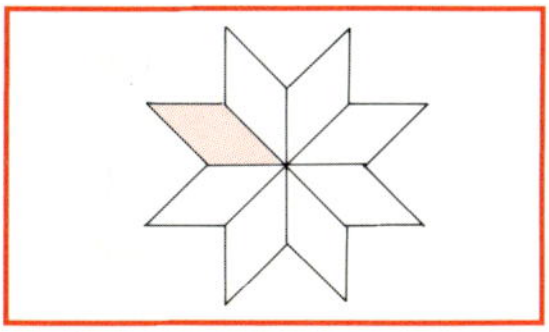

Eight-point star

Draw a line AB on a piece of template card or plastic, this will be the length of the diamond sides. Using a protractor, mark a line from point A at 45° to this line. Set a pair of compasses to the length of AB. Place the compass point at A and bisect the line above at C. Place the compass point at C and draw an arc. Place the compass point at B and bisect the arc. Join up the points to form a diamond used for an eight-point star.

Short diamonds

Work in exactly the same way as above but mark the second line at 60° to the first. This diamond is

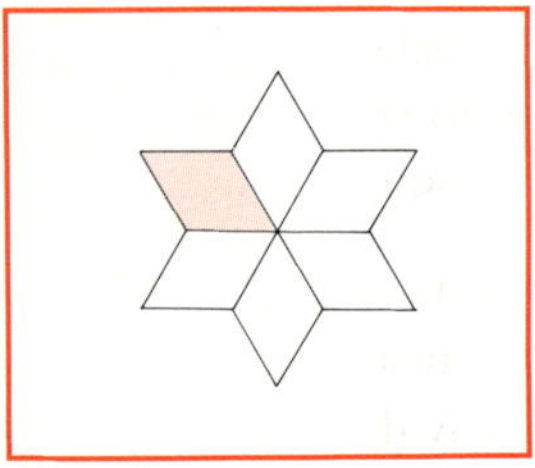

Six-point star

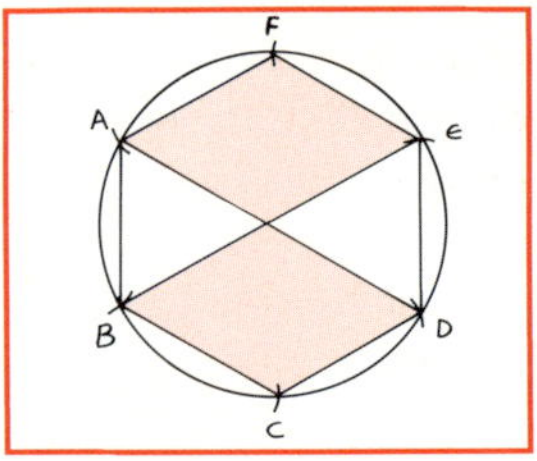

Short diamonds from a circle

used for the Baby Blocks design (see page 85) and for a six-point star.

Alternatively, draw a circle with a radius equal to the chosen length of the diamond sides. Draw up into a hexagon as described above, then join points A and B to the opposite points E and D. This will produce two diamonds and two equilateral triangles as well.

Half and quarter square triangles

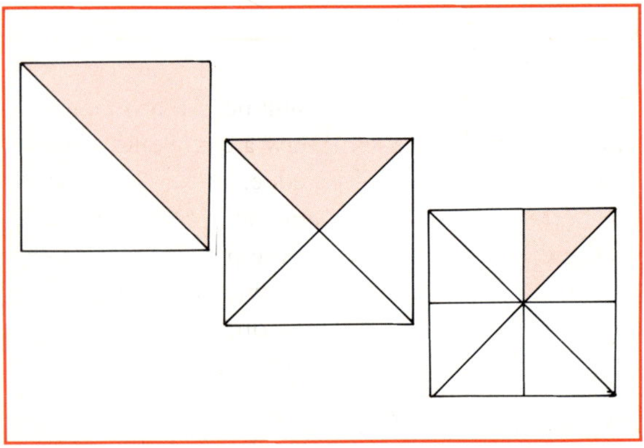

Half square, quarter square and eighth square triangles

Draw up a basic square. Use a ruler to mark a diagonal line from one corner to the opposite corner. This produces two half square triangles.

To mark a quarter square triangle, draw a line in the opposite direction dividing the first triangles in half again. This square can be subdivided again by drawing lines vertically and horizontally across the square: this will produce eight right-angled triangles.

Pentagon

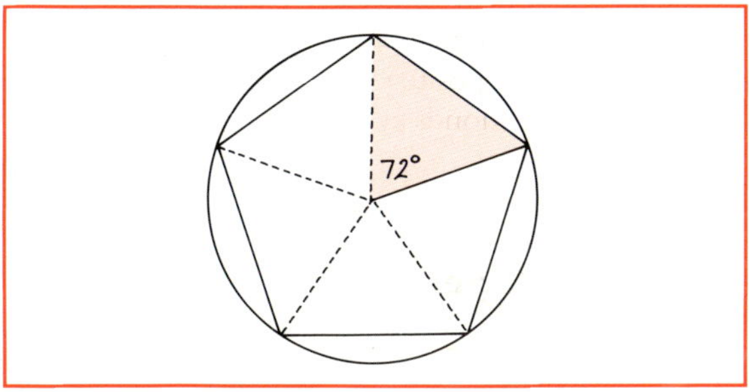

Constructing a hexagon

To draw this template you will need a protractor and a pair of compasses. Draw a circle and mark a line from the centre to the edge. Place the protractor on this line and mark a line at 72° from it, out to the circumference. Place the protractor on this new line and repeat. Repeat twice more, then join up the points to form a pentagon.

Octagon

Draw a circle to the desired size.

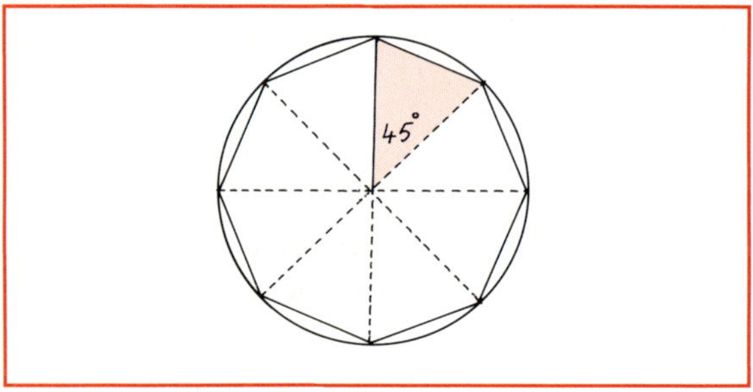

Constructing an octagon

Draw two diameters at right angles to each other. Draw two more diameters bisecting the right angles of the first two. Join up the points of the diameter.

Note: Templates can also be drawn on squared and isometric graph paper. Use squared graph paper for drawing squares and rectangles. By marking diagonal lines across squared paper, you can also draw triangles and octagons. Draw up hexagons, short diamonds and equilateral triangles on isometric graph paper.

Drafting Patchwork Patterns

Simple one-patch designs

These can be drawn up quickly onto squared or isometric graph paper. Only a small section of the finished article need be drawn to actual size, but a scaled down version of the whole design will be a help when plotting the colours and fabrics.

Two-patch designs

These are also quite easy to draw up in reduced format to gauge size and colour.

Block patchwork

For this a design plan is needed to map out the pattern, for deciding on the fabric colours and for choosing the size.

Draw up a square to the size of the finished block and mark out your chosen block design or divide the square with a grid and add your own design using a ruler and pencil. In some block designs the pattern follows the grid squares, in others some of the grid squares are bisected diagonally into triangular shapes (see page 88).

To draft a patchwork made up of only one block design, first draw up the chosen block at a reduced size on graph paper, then use tracing paper to trace more blocks and plot them over the graph paper, either in repeat form or by turning the blocks at different degrees (for example, as a mirror image). Once the design looks good, use crayons to fill in the colours, then draw up one block to the actual size. Use this actual-size block as a pattern for cutting the templates and as a guide for stitching the patchwork pieces together.

Variations in the design can be produced by alternating pieced blocks with plain ones and by turning each square so that it is resting on a corner rather than a side. This is called "setting on point".

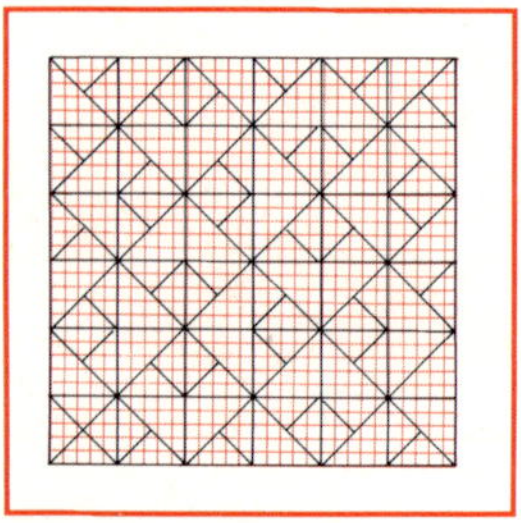

Mirror images

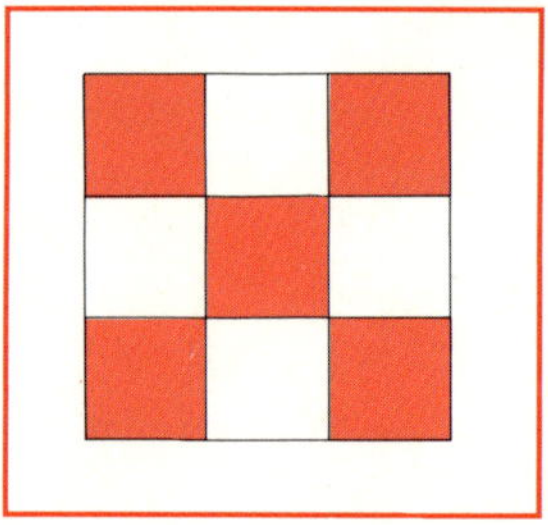

Plain and pieced blocks

Setting on point

Sashing and borders

Sashing or borders

These can also be used to great effect in a patchwork design. Redraw the block pattern placing a strip between each row of blocks, then mark a border around the edge. Sashing does not need to be plain, it can be pieced, and several borders can be added to increase the size and/or to add extra colour and pattern to the finished piece.

Pieced borders

These are best kept to simple repeat patterns. When putting a border design together, begin marking the design in the centre of each side and work out towards the corners.

Pieced border designs

Borders with corner squares

If the border design does not fit successfully in the corners, insert a small plain square.

TRADITIONAL ENGLISH PIECED PATCHWORK

In this hand-stitched method of patchwork the fabric patches are cut out with a ¼in (5mm) allowance all around, then a paper patch or lining is cut out 1/4in (5mm) smaller than each fabric patch. The allowance on the fabric patch is folded in all around the paper lining and tacked in place. The paper linings help to retain the shape and give the fabric body while the patches are stitched together. They are removed after all the patches have been joined. The various stages in making this patchwork are described below.

This type of patchwork is very accurate and produces a strong fabric. The shapes are generally hexagons and diamonds.

Cutting the paper linings

Each fabric patch must have a paper lining or template.

1 Fold the paper or layer several sheets together so several templates can be cut at the same time.

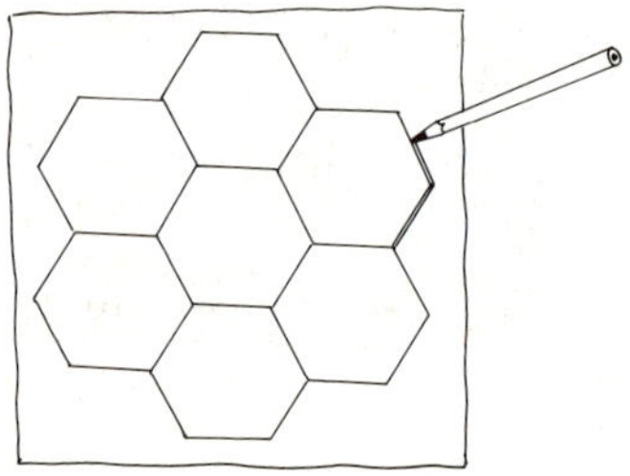

Marking out the paper linings

2 If using a pair of templates (see page 13), lay the smaller metal template on the paper and draw around with a sharp pencil. Alternatively, use a specially-made lining template in the same way. Repeat as many times as necessary.

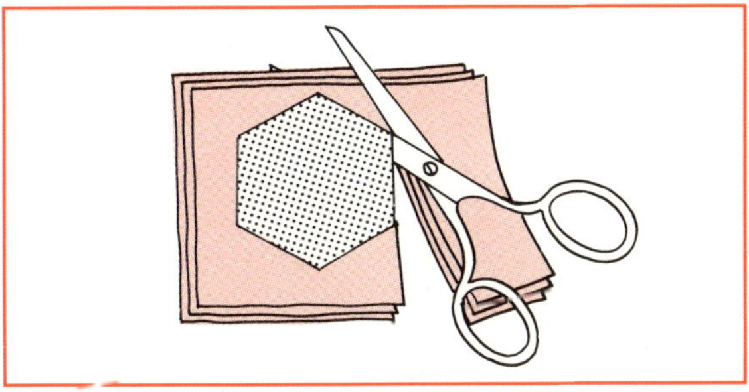

Cutting the paper linings

3 Holding the paper layers firmly together, carefully cut out the shapes, either with a sharp pair of paper scissors, rotary cutter or sharp craft knife held against a metal ruler.

Cutting the fabric patches

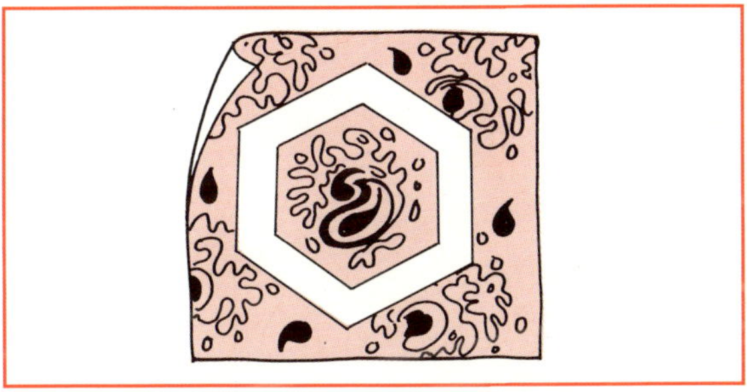

Centring a design within a window template

Place the window template on the right side of the fabric and move it about until the chosen section of the fabric is shown in the central window. Line up two straight edges of the template with the straight grain of the fabric. Holding the template firmly, mark around the outer edge with tailors' chalk or marking pencil. Carefully cut out. If using a card template, the siting of the motif will not be quite so easy to judge.

Making up the patches

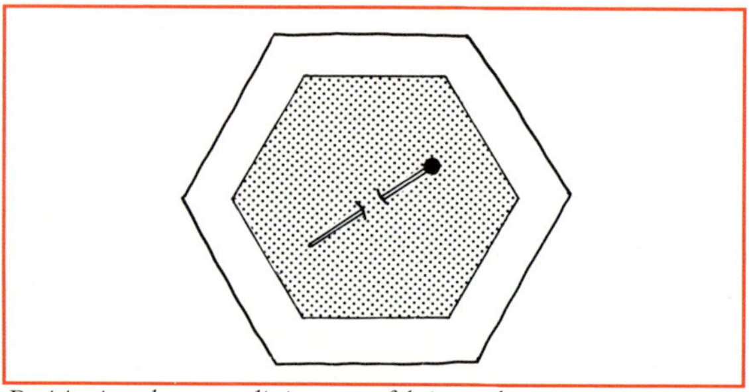

Positioning the paper lining on a fabric patch

1 Place a paper lining centrally to the wrong side of a fabric patch; hold firmly in place with pins across the centre.

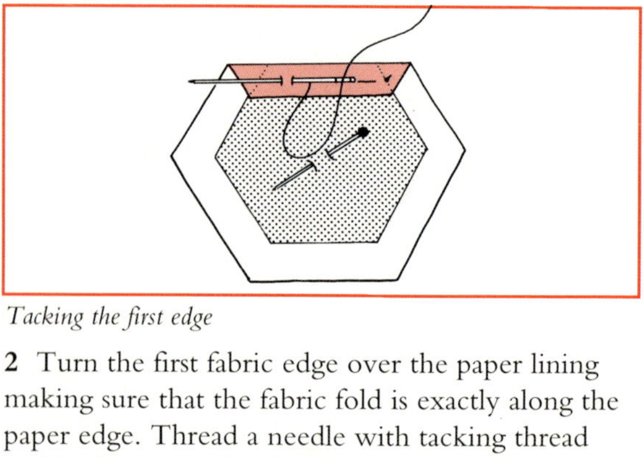

Tacking the first edge

2 Turn the first fabric edge over the paper lining making sure that the fabric fold is exactly along the paper edge. Thread a needle with tacking thread and beginning with a backstitch to secure the thread, tack in place through all three layers, seam allowance, paper and front of patch.

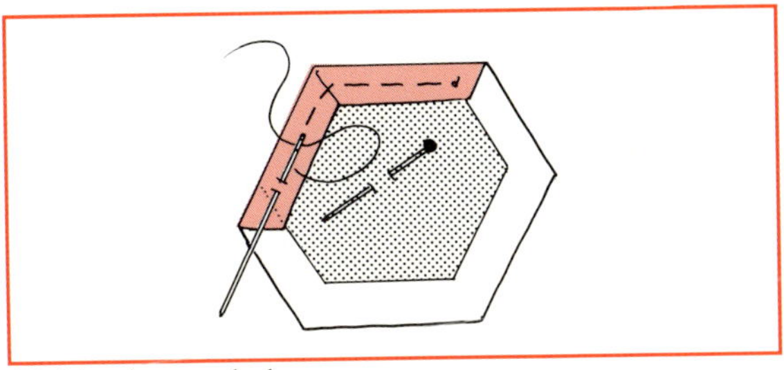

Tacking the second edge

3 When you reach the first corner, fold over the next edge in the same way and tack in place. Repeat all around the shape, ending with another backstitch.

4 When all the patches are prepared, press well.

Joining the patches together

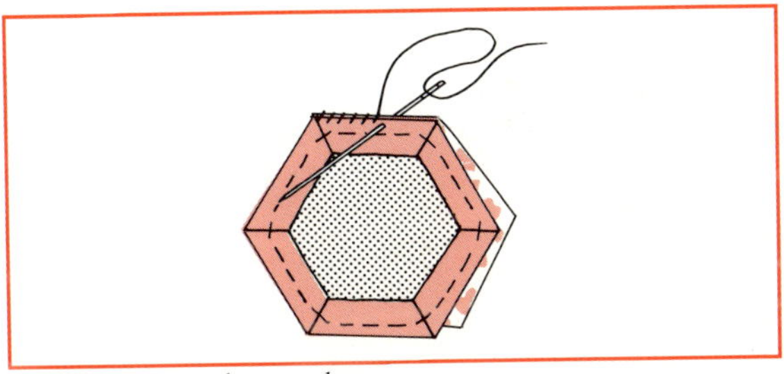

Stitching two patches together

1 Place the first two patches, back to back, with right sides together, exactly matching all edges. Thread a fine Betweens needle with a neutral-coloured thread and fasten it into the fabric with two or three backstitches worked on the spot through the seam allowance near the first corner. Stitch the two patches together with tiny overcasting stitches along one edge. Only pick up one or two threads of each fabric with each stitch. Do not stitch through the paper. Fasten the thread at the end with a couple of backstitches worked on the spot through the seam allowance.

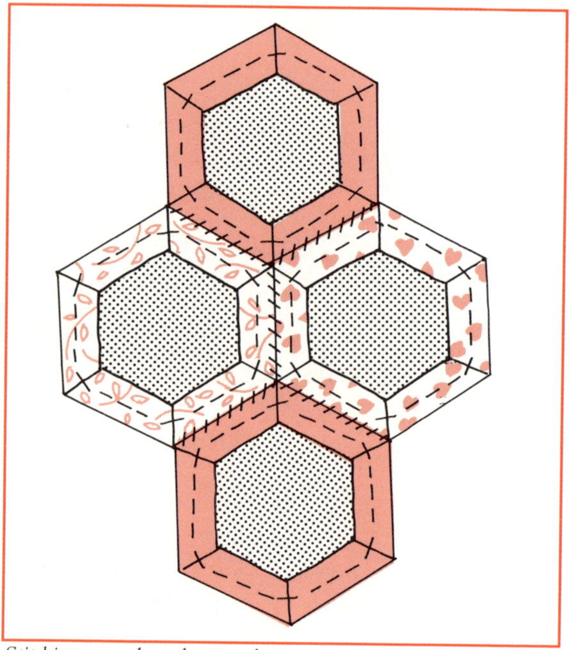

Stitching several patches together

2 Flatten the patches and check that the stitches are almost invisible. Join the remaining patches to the first two in the same way, stitching one or two adjoining sides together at a time.

3 When all the patches are joined together, flatten them out and press well. Carefully remove the tacking threads and paper linings, then press again.

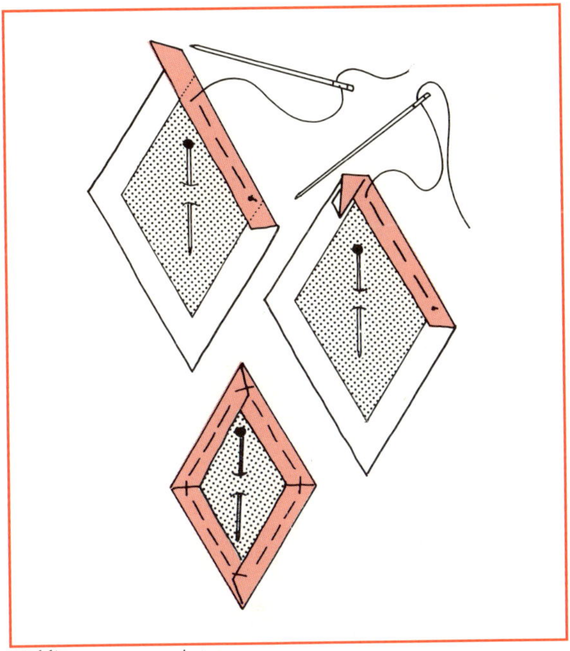

Folding an acute point

4 When sewing diamond and triangle shapes together the acute point must be folded down in two movements to gain a good point of fabric.

Note: The patches can be joined by machine using a zigzag stitch, but skill is needed to just catch a few threads of each fabric along the edges.

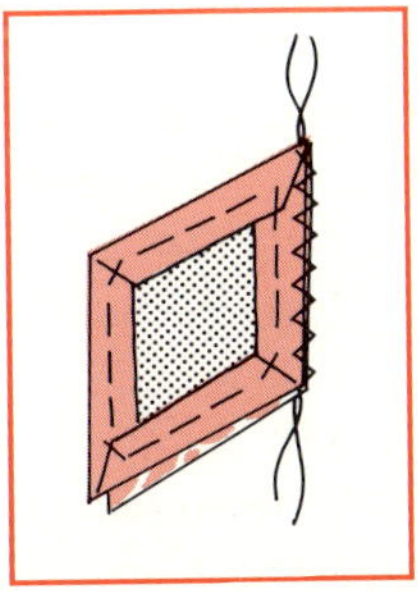

American Block Patchwork

This method is much quicker as there are no paper linings. Block designs can be quickly built up using straight sided shapes, such as squares, rectangles and triangles. Once the blocks have been formed they can be stitched together or divided by bands, called sashing or lattice, and completed with bound edges.

Cutting with a rotary cutter

A rotary cutter speeds up the process of cutting templates enormously. It can also be used in conjunction with a number of commercial measuring devices to produce accurate fabric patches without the need of a template.

As well as the rotary cutter you will need a self-healing cutting mat and a set square.

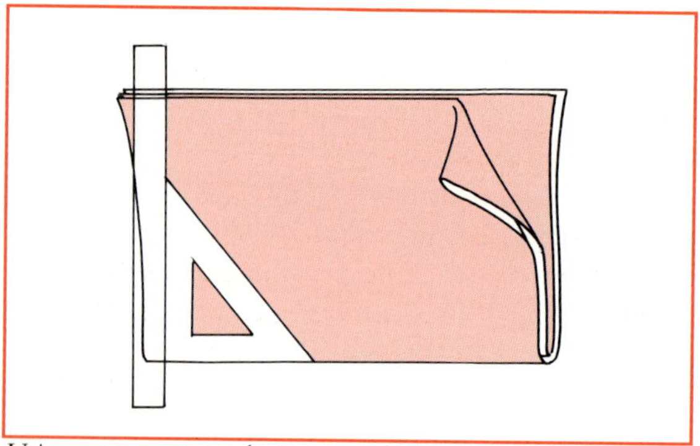

Using a set square to obtain a straight edge

1 Fold the fabric lengthwise, matching selvages, then fold again matching the fold to the selvages. Line the bottom edge of the set square up with the fabric edge and place the ruler against the adjacent edge.

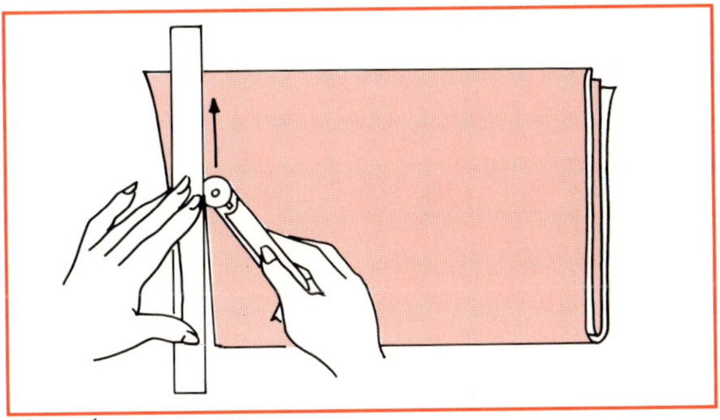

Using the rotary cutter

2 Holding the ruler firmly, remove the triangle. Position the blade of the rotary cutter against the ruler and run it along the ruler's edge, pushing the blade away from you. This will give you a straight edge cut with the straight of the grain. Repeat, to cut as many strips as necessary. The strips can then be cut into the required shapes.

Cutting the fabric patches

1 Cut the template to the finished size. Place the template on the wrong side of the fabric, making sure that it lies on the straight of the grain. Mark around the template using a marking pen or soft pencil. Leaving 1/2in (1cm) between this patch and the next one, mark out as many patches as you need.

2 When working with squares or rectangles you can use a ruler and a pencil to mark out the shapes on the wrong side of the fabric. In this case use a set square to make sure that you mark all the squares on the straight of the grain. Again leave a margin of 1/2in (1cm) between each patch.

3 Cut out with a 1/4in (5mm) allowance all around each patch.

Joining the patches by machine

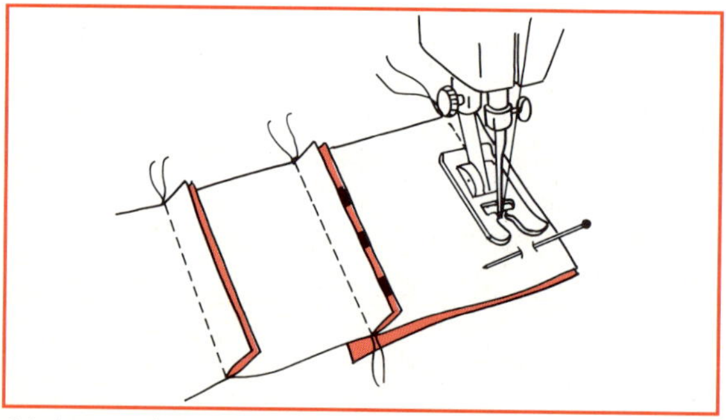

Machine stitching the patches

1 Pin the first two patches back to back, with right sides together. Straight stitch on the machine between the seam allowances following the pencil lines.

2 To make up a block, pin and stitch the patches together into vertical strips. When you have the correct number of strips for the block, pin and stitch the strips together to form the block. Pin across the seamlines to make sure that they match exactly.

Joining the patches by hand

Before sewing machines were widely available, American needlewomen hand stitched their patchwork pieces together. Instead of using the English method of oversewing, they used a running stitch, which made the transition to the sewing machine very straightforward.

1 Place the first two patches back to back, with right sides together. Pin at right angles to the stitching line, placing a pin through each corner point first, then at intervals in between.

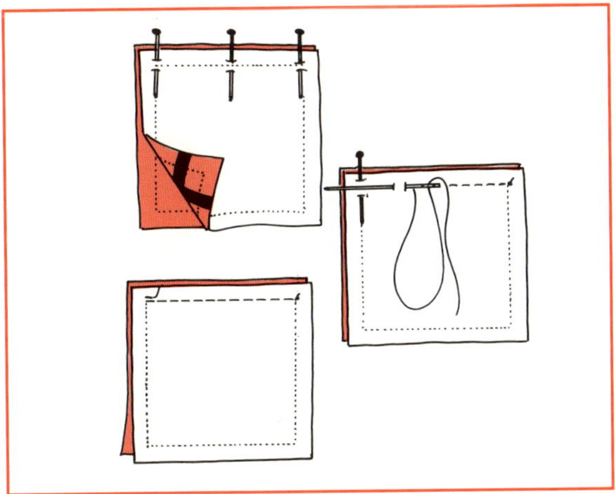

Hand stitching the patches

2 Thread a fine Betweens needle with a 15in(38cm) length of sewing cotton and insert at the corner point. Stitch across the seam following the marked stitching line. Check that the stitches run along the marked line on the wrong side as well. Do not stitch into the seam allowances. Finish at the opposite corner point with two or three back stitches.

Stitching the rows together

When the patches have been joined together into rows, these rows can be stitched together to form the patchwork.

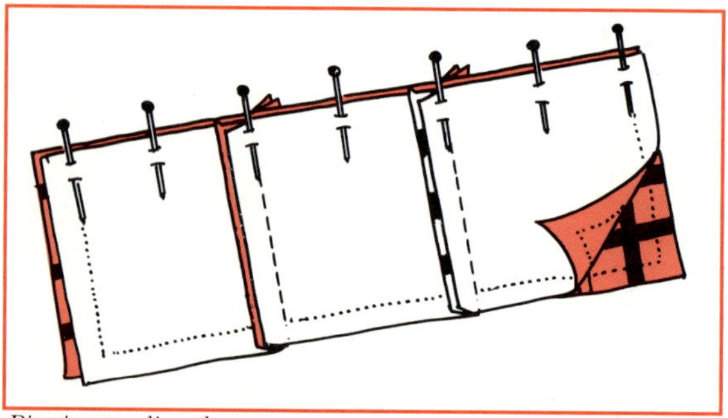

Pinning to align the seams

1 Place the first two rows back to back with right sides together. Position a pin at the end of each row and where the seams meet. Add extra pins as needed in between.

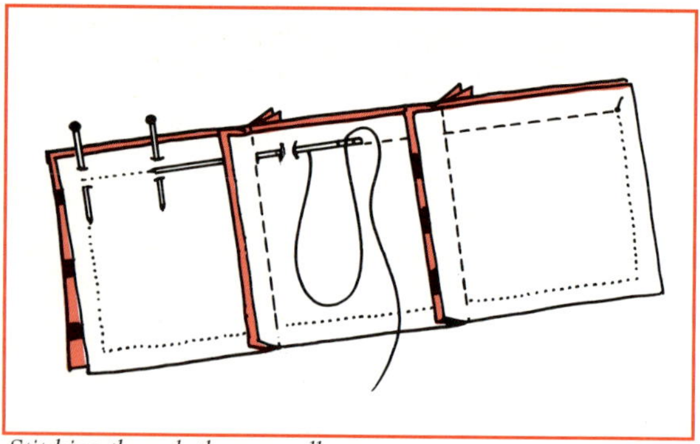

Stitching through the seam allowance

2 Stitch along the marked stitching line with small running stitches in the same way as above. Do not stitch through the seam allowances, instead, when you reach a seam, work a backstitch, then take the needle through the seam allowance to the other side. Work another backstitch, then continue stitching the seam.

3 Join the strips together in sections to avoid handling large areas of fabric until the final steps.

Stitching a curved seam (as in Drunkard's Path)

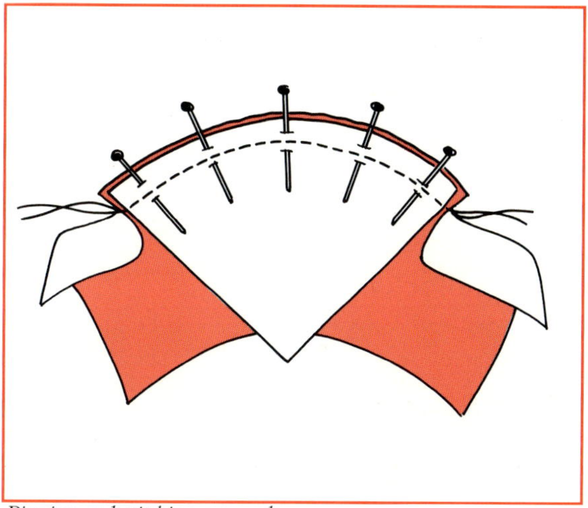

Pinning and stitching a curved seam

1 Staystitch around the inner curve. Snip into the seam allowance.

2 Place the inward curve to the outward curve, right sides together. Pin and stitch around the curved seam, gently easing the inward seam open to fit around the outward curve.

Chain piecing

To save time, squares can be stitched together in a row. Place the pieces together in pairs. Feed them

Chain piecing pairs of patches

through the sewing machine, one after the other without breaking the thread. When the row is complete, cut between the squares to separate them.

Joining blocks with sashing

The completed patchwork blocks can be joined together with dividing strips, called sashing or lattice, spaced either into vertical strips or horizontally and vertically. Take 1/4in (5mm) seam allowance when stitching the blocks together.

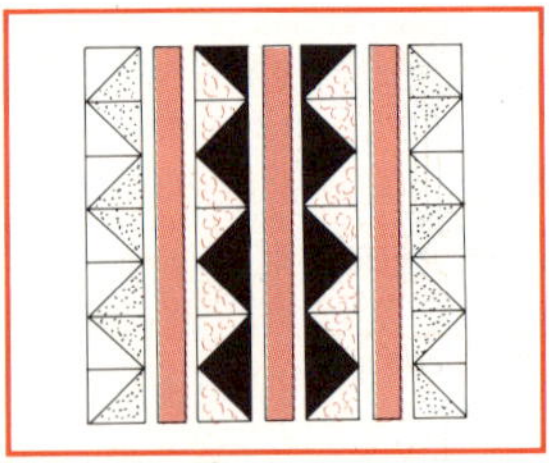

Vertical sashing

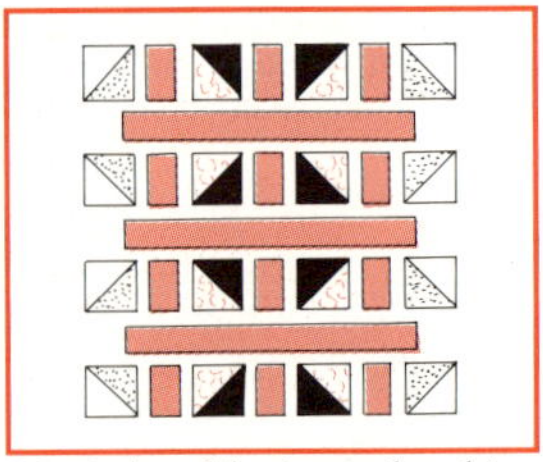

Vertical and horizontal sashing

To add vertical sashing, pin and stitch the blocks together into vertical lengths matching edges exactly. Measure the length of the finished strips and cut a piece of sashing to fit between each block strip, adding a 1/4in (5mm) seam allowance on either side of the finished width of the sashing. Pin and stitch the sashing between the block strips. Make sure the block seams match the sashing strips horizontally.

To add horizontal and vertical sashing, join the blocks horizontally with block length sashing between each block. When the horizontal rows of blocks are complete, measure the width and cut horizontal sashing to this width plus seam allowances. Pin and stitch the sashing in between the horizontal rows of blocks.

Order of piecing blocks

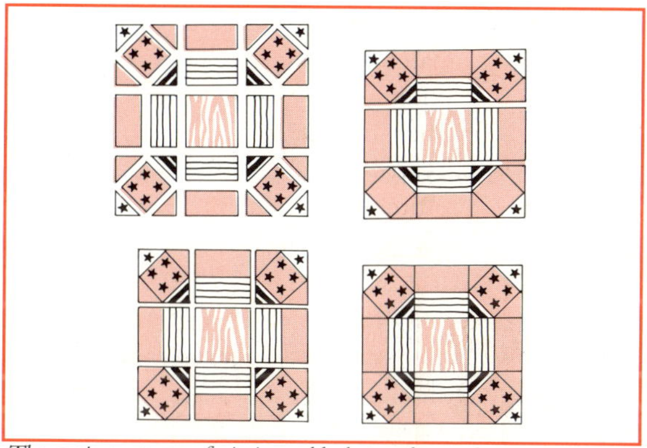

The various stages of piecing a block together

After cutting out all the pieces, lay them on a flat surface in the correct order to plan how to stitch them together. The best way is to make up the small pieces into larger units, then join these larger units into rows and finally, the rows into a block. In machine stitched patchwork, try to keep all the seams straight.

Pressing seams

Always press all connecting seams before joining the next piece.

Press machine stitched seams open. Press on the wrong side first, then on the right side over a cloth to prevent glazing.

When stitching patchwork by hand, the seams will be stronger if the seams are pressed to one side. Either press all the seams towards the darker of the patches, or press all the seams in the same direction.

Press each block or section after it has been completed, then press the rows as they are joined. This will help to keep the blocks of an even size and make pressing the final patchwork a lot easier.

Other Kinds of Patchwork

Cathedral window patchwork

This patchwork is based on a background of folded squares of fabric. When two squares are stitched together a square of contrasting fabric is placed diagonally over the join. The central square is held in place by the turned back edges of the background fabric creating a frame.

1 From the backing fabric, cut out 6in (15cm) squares on the straight of the grain. Mark across each square both ways to mark the centre.

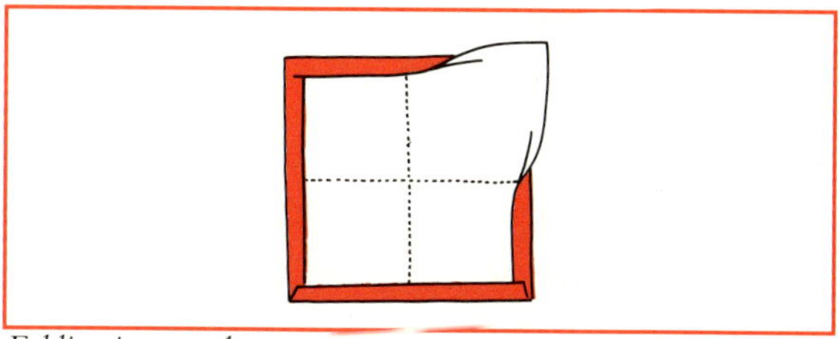

Folding in raw edge

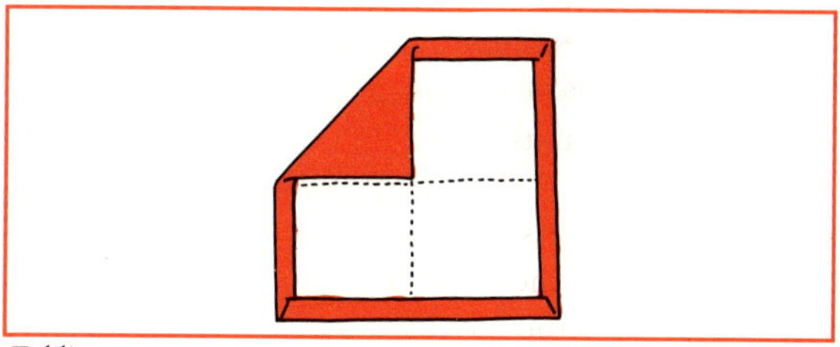

Folding corner to centre

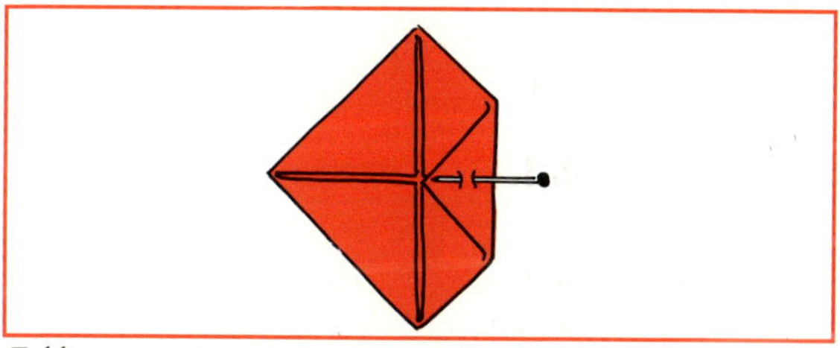

Folding corner to centre again

2 Turn in and press 1/4in (5mm) all around each square.

3 Fold in each corner to the centre point; press and pin to form a 3 3/4in (9.5cm) square.

4 Fold each corner into the centre again, to form a 2 5/8in (6.5cm) square; press and pin.

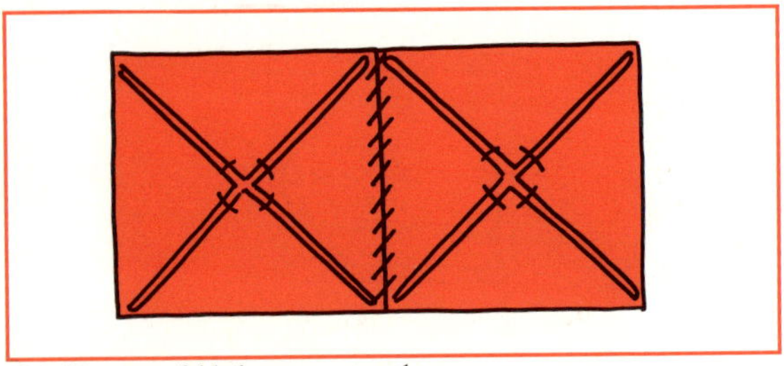

Stitching two folded squares together

5 Thread a fine needle with a neutral colour thread and stab stitch through the four centre points to hold them together. Fasten off the thread at the back.

6 Make up all the squares in the same way. Place two squares with turned-in sides together. Thread a fine needle with a neutral-coloured cotton. Begin with a couple of back stitches, then oversew the two edges together with small neat oversewing stitches. End with a couple of back stitches.

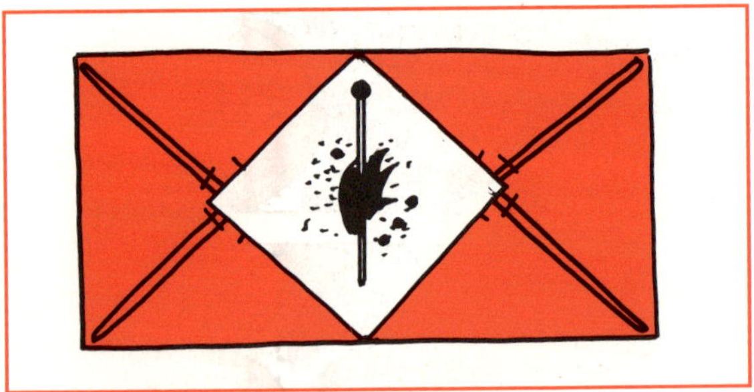

Positioning the contrasting "window"

7 Open the squares out flat. Cut a 1 1/2in (4cm) square of contrasting fabric. Pin this square diagonally over the oversewn join between the two background squares.

Rolling back and stitching the edges

8 On each side of the square, beginning in the centre of the folded edge, roll back the folded edge of the backing fabric over the raw edges of central square for about 1/8in (3mm) tapering off to a neat point at each end. Fasten a neutral thread with a double back stitch worked on the spot at each end across the converging sides, then stitch through all layers with running stitches. Continue joining backing squares together and adding central squares in the same way until the size required.

Alternative treatments for the corners

9 Half squares on the outer edges can either be left as they are or the edge of the backing squares can be rolled back and stitched for decorative effect.

This type of patchwork automatically produces a neat back and sides but borders can be added if required for reasons of size or effect (see page 76).

Clamshell or Shell patchwork

An unusual patchwork shape, the clamshell is based on a circle. It is also sometimes called "Fishscale patchwork" as the shapes overlap like the scales of a fish. The overall effect depends on a good arrangement of plain and patterned fabrics or light and dark colours, so that the individual shapes are distinguished from each other. There are two methods of constructing the clamshell patches.

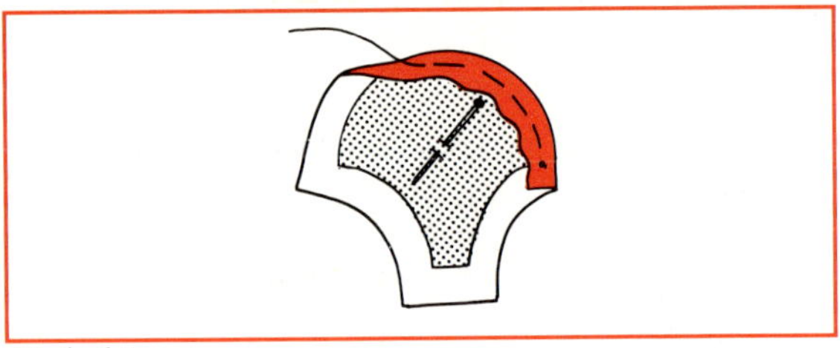

Method 1

Method 1: Each patch is formed around a lining of iron-on interfacing.

1 Use a clamshell template to cut out as many linings from iron-on interfacing as necessary.

2 Place the template on the wrong side of the fabric on the straight of the grain and mark around. Leaving a 1/4in (5mm) margin all around the outline, cut out as many patches as you need.

3 Position the interfacing template centrally on the wrong side of a fabric patch and iron to fix in place. Turn over the seam allowance around the curved edge; pin. Thread a fine needle with a neutral tacking cotton and, beginning with a back stitch, tack around the curved edge. Press the patch firmly. Remove the pins. Repeat with the rest of the patches.

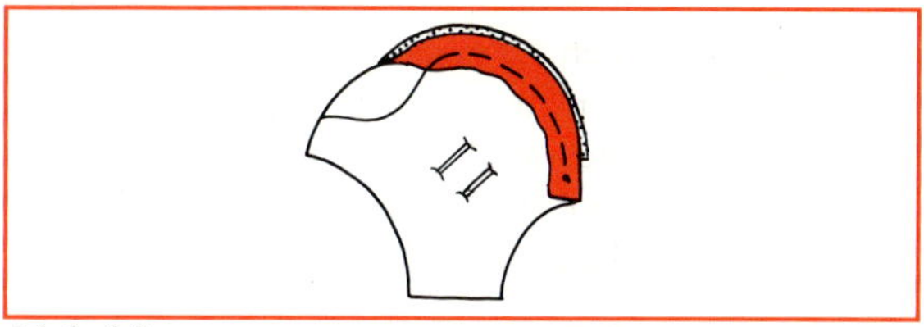

Method 2

Method 2: Each patch is formed using a thin card template.

1 Cut several clamshell templates in thin card or stiff paper.

2 Place one of the card templates on the wrong side of the fabric on the straight of the grain. Leaving a 1/4in (5mm) margin all around the outline, cut out as many patches as you need.

3 Now place a card template centrally on the right side of a fabric patch. Secure with two pins.

4 Turn over the curved top edge of the fabric patch to the wrong side, using the card template as a guide only and pleating the fullness of the fabric. Thread a fine needle with a neutral tacking cotton and, beginning with a back stitch, tack around the curved edge, without stitching into the card template. Remove the card template. Press the patch firmly. Repeat with the rest of the patches.

Assembling the patches

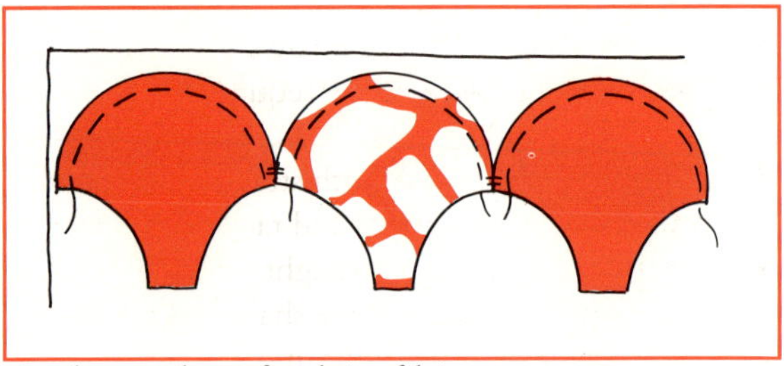

Attaching patches to foundation fabric

1 To assemble the patchwork, cut a piece of foundation fabric to the size of the finished piece of patchwork. Place a row of clamshells side by side across the top edge of the foundation fabric, with side edges butting together. Check that the top curved edges of each shape are in a straight line. Tack in place. Thread a fine needle with a length of neutral thread and fasten the shells together at each side with a couple of backstitches.

2 Place the second row of patches overlapping the seam allowance of the stems of the first row, so the curved top edges fall in between two clamshells of the first row and raw edges are hidden. Pin, tack and backstitch as before. Carefully hemstitch around the curved edges through all layers.

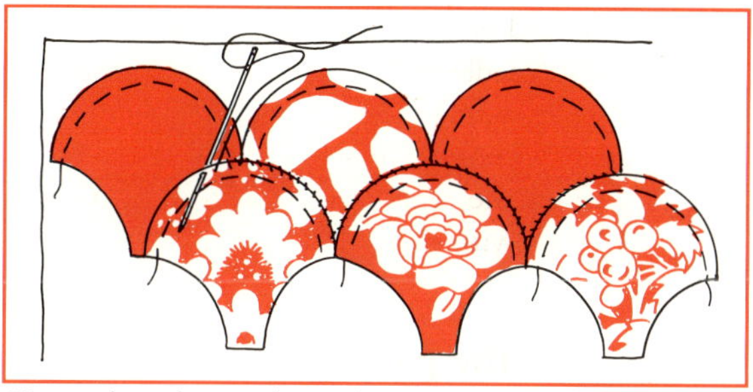

Hemstitching the second row of patches

3 Repeat to stitch subsequent rows in the same way until the patchwork is the required size.

4 To finish the patchwork with straight edges,either fold under the curved shapes and tack to the back or cut off the top edge in a straight line halfway down the patches and use these shapes to fill in the corresponding gaps at the bottom edge. Do the same at the side edges. Remove tacking stitches.

Crazy patchwork

The Victorians loved to mix silks and satins and velvets together in their crazy patchwork pieces. However if the item needs to be practical as well as colourful, only mix together richly-coloured cottons and silks. The best way of making up a sizeable area of crazy patchwork is to cut the foundation fabric into squares of workable size and after applying the patches seam them together as blocks with or without sashing. These bands of plain fabric can help balance and contain the vibrant groups of fabric pieces.

1 Wash and iron the foundation fabric and press.

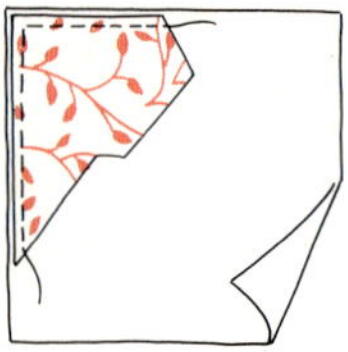

Attaching the first crazy patch

2 Cut into squares. Sort the patches into light and dark tones and decide on the size of the pieces in relation to the foundation square and the finished article. Choose ten or twelve patches and move them about the foundation square to gauge the effect, when the result looks good, pin them in place, beginning in one corner and overlapping each piece.

3 When the arrangement has been pinned, trim off any fabric underneath an overlapping patch to 1/8in (3mm) and tack all around the patches, tucking under 1/4in (5mm) hem on all exposed edges.

4 Working by hand with a small running stitch or by machine with a straight stitch, stitch all around each patch close to folded edge. Check that all the layers have been stitched together.

Stitching around the foundation piece

Decorating with surface embroidery

5 Embroidery can be worked over the folded edges. Either work machine embroidery stitches or free style stitches, such as herringbone or feather stitch.

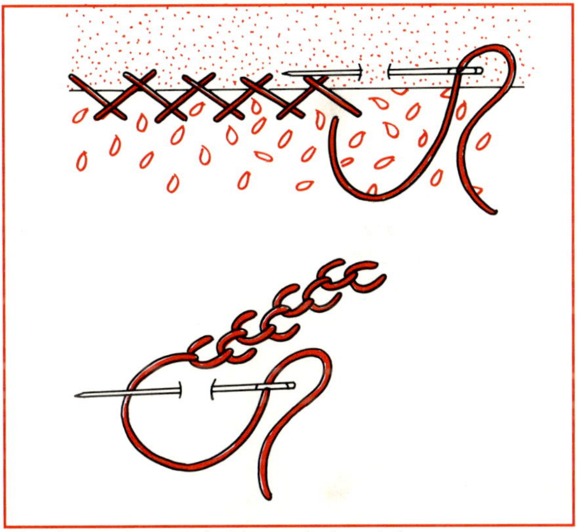

Top: herrringbone stitch; bottom: feather stitch

6 When the embroidery is complete, pin and stitch the separate blocks together to form one piece, with or without border and sashing.

Double wedding ring

Five templates are used for this pattern, two for the background fabrics, two to make the arcs of the rings and the fifth template is used to cut the patches which connect every four arcs.

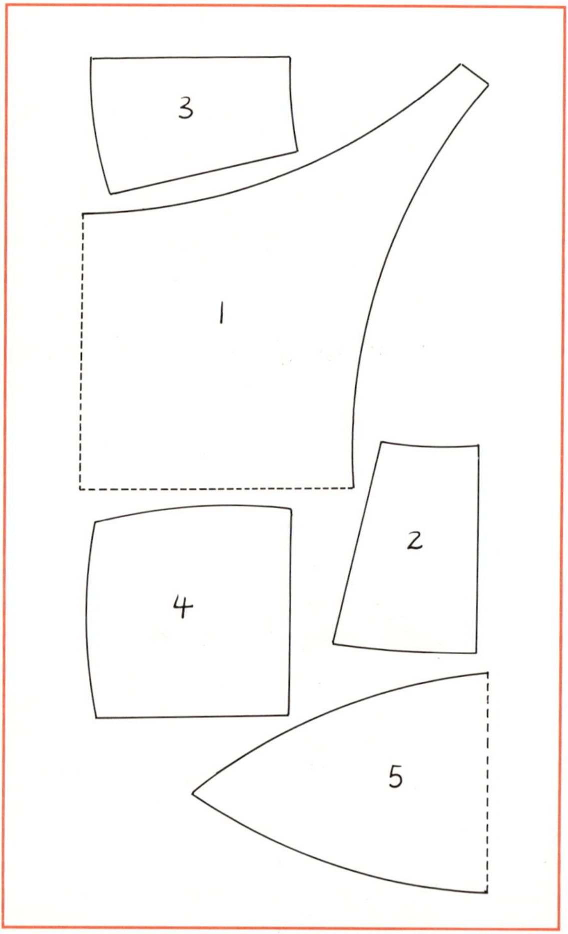

1 Trace and enlarge the templates to the size required. Note that only half of template 5 is shown and a quarter of template 1. Place the dotted lines against a folded edge. For each "ring", cut out one centre background shape and four centre arc shapes. Mark the centres of each piece. For the

Assembling the two arcs

four arcs cut twenty-four template 3 patches and eight template 2 patches for each end.

2 To make up each arc, pin and stitch six template 3 patches together with a template 2 patch at either end. Press the seams all one way. Make up a

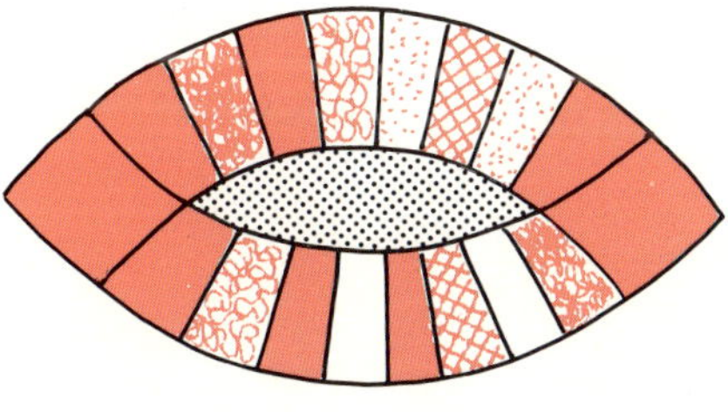

Joining the arcs to the background section

second arc in the same way, adding the larger template 4 patch at each end.

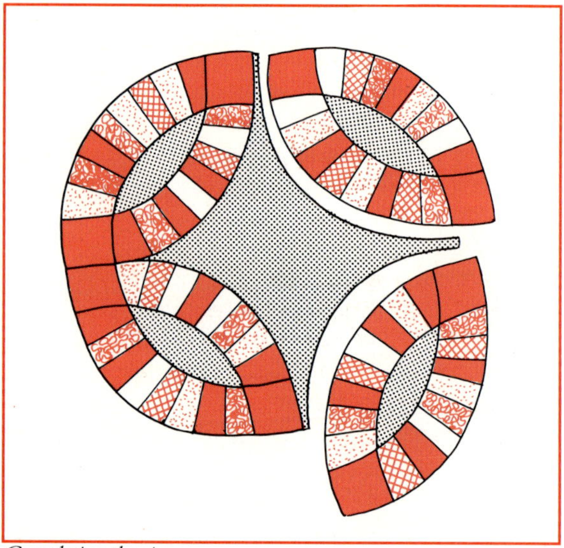

Completing the ring

3 Pin and stitch each arc around one of the four background sections, attach the smaller arc first, matching centre points, then adding the second arc.

4 Matching centres, place the arcs to each edge of the centre background piece; pin and stitch in place working clockwise around the background shapes. When the ring is complete, press the seam allowances away from the central background shape.

5 Make up as many rings as you need, then join the rings together using the large background shapes. Pin and stitch into rows alternating rings with background shapes, then join the rows in the same way. On the outside edges, add another arc shape, and to complete the ring effect, add two at each corner.

Log cabin patchwork

Log cabin patchwork is built up from straight sided strips. You do not need templates, but the strips need to be cut to the same width. The strips can be cut to the correct length as you stitch. The strips are stitched together onto a foundation square and traditionally made up of equal numbers of light and dark strips, graduating out from a central square. Plan small items on a foundation piece approximately 6in (15cm) square; for larger items cut the squares between 12 and 16in (30 and 40cm).

The following instructions are for a large square - cut the strips 1½in (4cm) wide for a small square.

1 Cut out the foundation square including a ¼in (5mm) seam allowance all around; fold in half diagonally both ways and mark the lines.

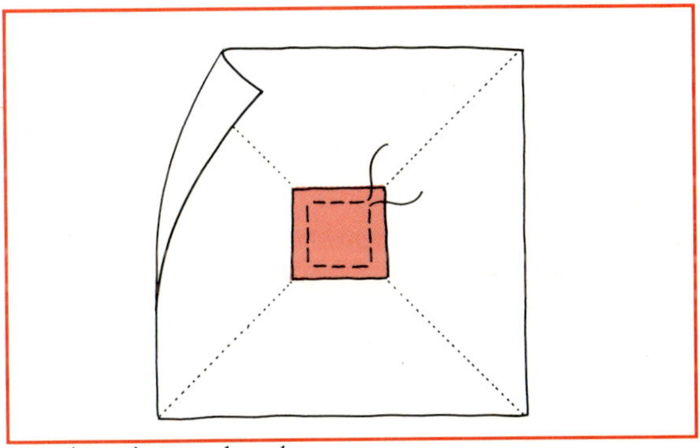

Attaching the central patch

2 Cut out the central patch approximately 2in (5cm) square - the same width as the strips - and, matching centres, tack in the centre of the foundation square.

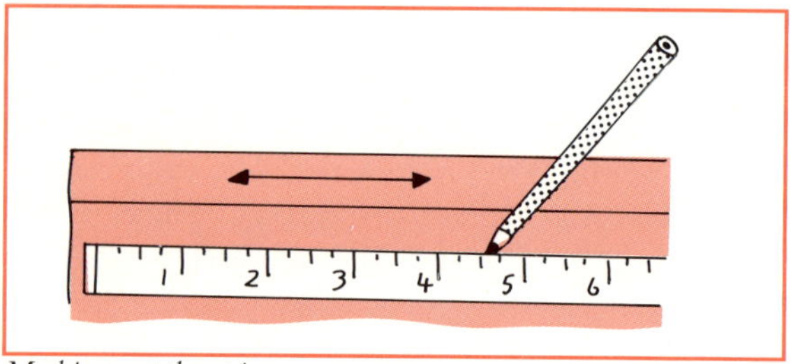

Marking out the strips

3 Work out how many strips of each fabric you need. Straighten the edge of the fabric first (see page 32), then using a ruler and soft pencil or marking pen, mark the 2in (5cm) wide strips on the wrong side of the fabric. Cut out each strip along the straight of the grain.

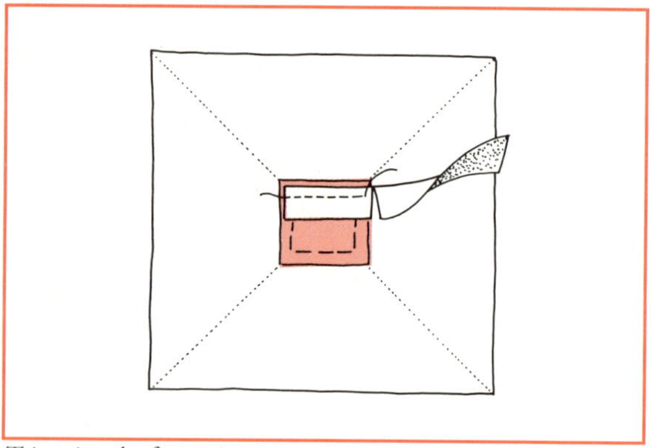

Trimming the first strip

4 Lay the first light strip over the central square with right sides facing. Machine stitch to the central square leaving a 1/4in (5mm) seam. Trim level with the edge of the central square. Turn the strip to the right side and press flat against the foundation square.

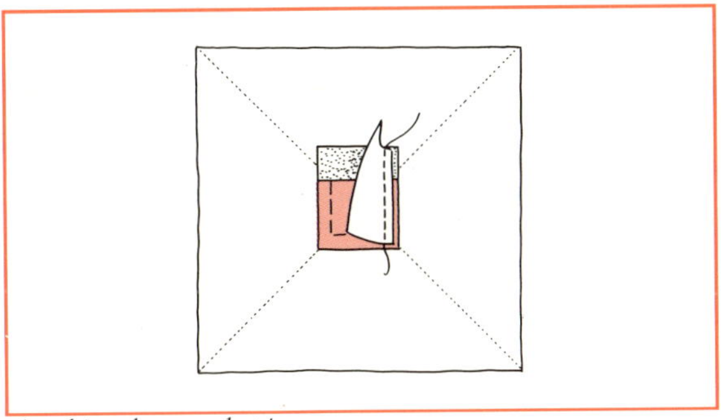

Attaching the second strip

5 Pin and stitch the next light coloured strip to the right of the central square continuing stitching across the end of the first strip. Trim level with the edge of the central square, turn the strip to the right side and press flat against the foundation square.

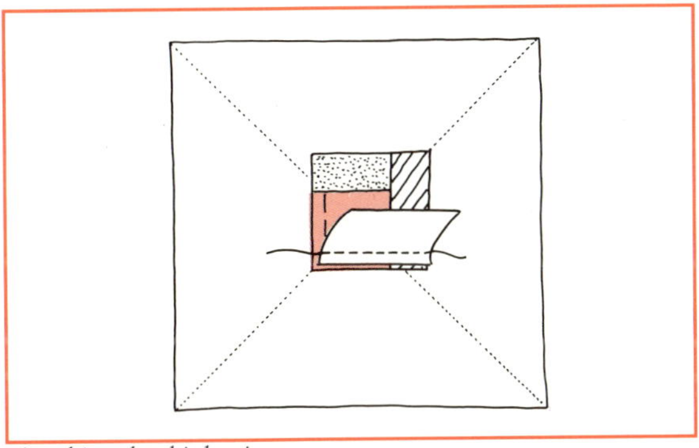

Attaching the third strip

6 Pin and stitch the first dark coloured strip to the base edge of the central square and over the end of the second strip. Trim and turn to the right side, then pin and stitch the second dark strip to the left-hand side of the central square and over the end of the first and fourth strip.

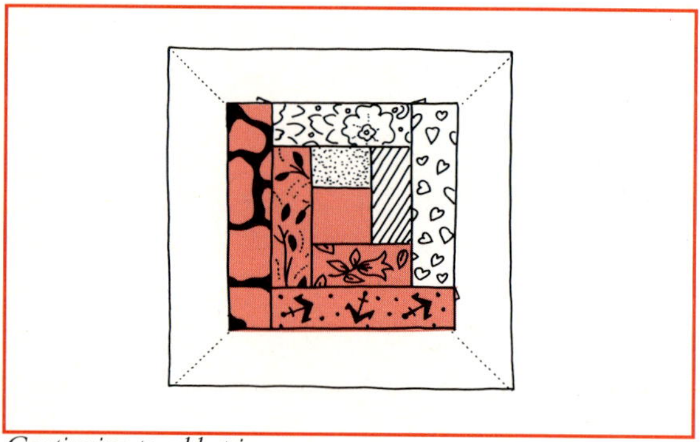

Continuing to add strips

7 Continue stitching and trimming the strips to the square with light coloured strips on one side and dark strips on the diagonally opposite edges. When the square is complete, tack the raw edges of the final strips to the foundation squares. Press well.

8 Make up as many squares as you need, then pin and stitch the squares together to form a larger pattern, positioning the light and dark sides so as to form the overall design.

Some classic arrangements are shown in the diagrams opposite.

Barn Raising

Diagonals

Dark and Light Squares

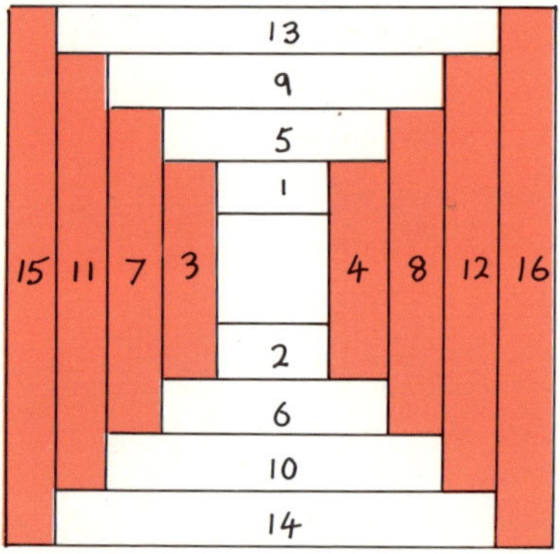

Order of attaching strips for "Courthouse steps"

Courthouse steps

This is a variation of Log Cabin. Strips are added in the proportions and sequence shown in the diagram, with light and dark squares on opposing sides of the square.

"Pineapple" variation

Pineapple (Windmill blades)

Another variation of Log Cabin, this design is for an experienced patchworker. The centre is composed of triangles, from which shaped strips radiate out in bands of light and dark fabrics.

Mariner's compass

A block design in which each "compass" is composed of five templates set inside a plain square made up of one template.

1 Trace and enlarge templates 1 to 6. Mark the templates on the wrong side of the fabric with a stitching line 1/4in (5mm) in from the edge all around. For each square cut one template 1 patch, four template 2 patches, four template 3 patches, eight template 4 patches, sixteen template 5 patches and four template 6 patches.

2 To assemble each square, follow the sequence shown in the diagrams on page 61.

3 For the circular centre, cut a patch from stiff paper using template 1 but omitting the seam allowance. Place the paper circle in the centre of the wrong side of the fabric circle and pin. Run a gathering thread around the seam and pull up so that the seam allowance is drawn over the paper circle. Press, then position this circle over the pieced square and hem stitch invisibly in place. Remove the paper insert.

Repeat as necessary for additional blocks.

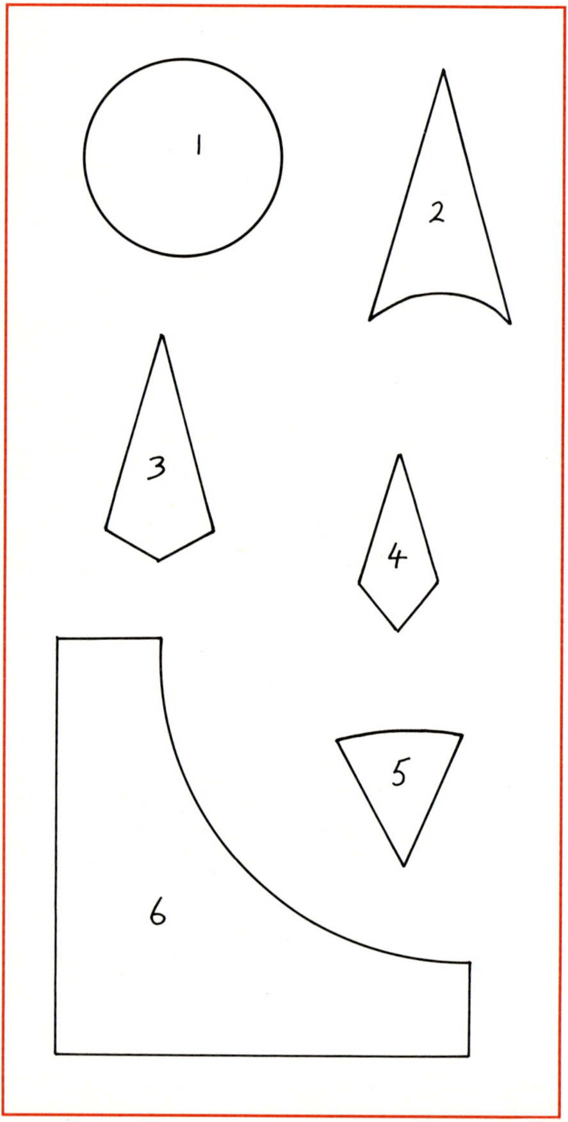
1
2
3
4
5
6

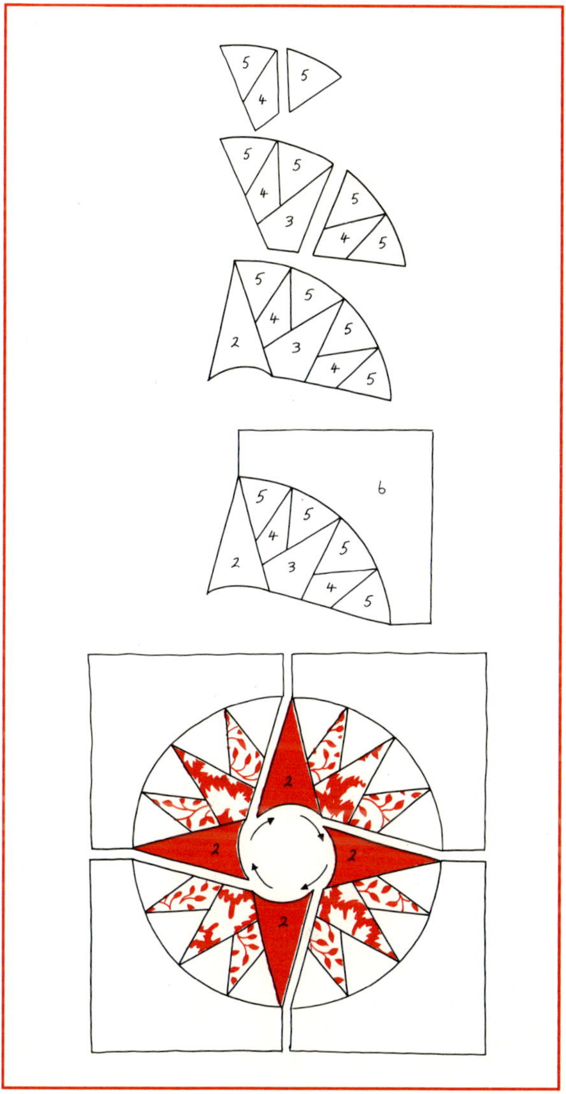

Order of assembly for one block

Padded patchwork

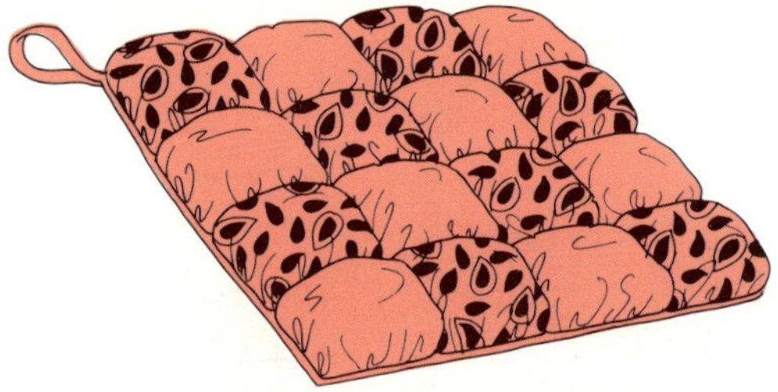

A padded potholder

Individual squares of fabric are seamed together and filled with padding. Pleats in each edge create the space for the filling and produce a rounded surface. The patches are stitched together creating a padded surface.

1 For each padded square you need a base and a top layer. For the base cut a 3 $^{1}/_{2}$in (9cm) square of fabric. For the top cut a 4 $^{3}/_{4}$in (12cm) square of fabric.

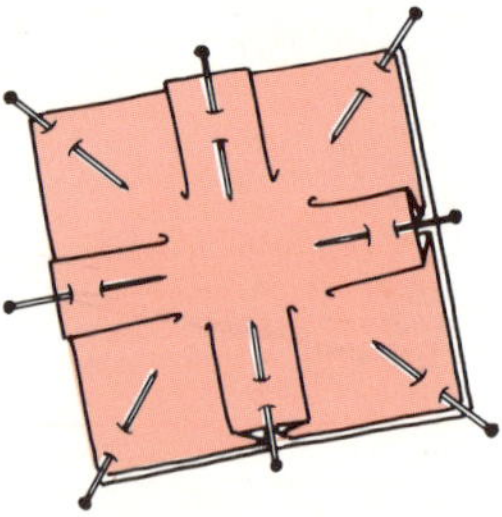

Pinning the top to the base

2 Mark the centre of each edge of the top piece. Place the top to the base, wrong sides together. On each edge of the top, fold the excess fabric into two even pleats and pin.

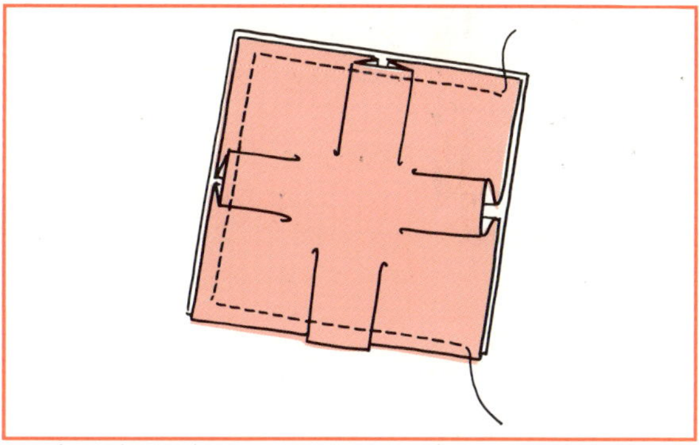

Stitching three sides

3 Stitch all around three sides taking 1/4in (5mm) seam allowance. Fill the puff to achieve a gently rounded top, then stitch across the remaining side. Repeat as necessary for additional blocks.

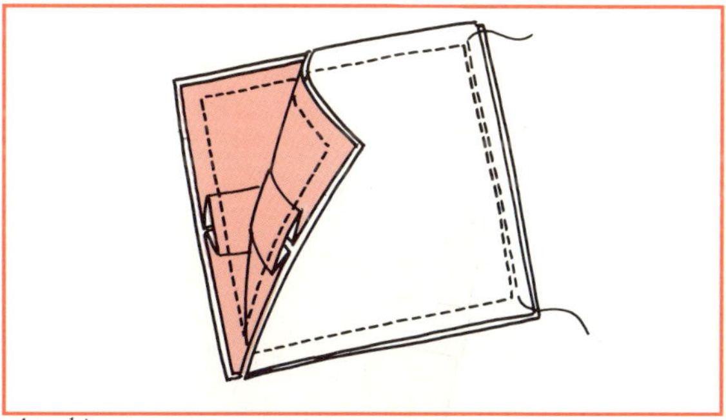

Attaching two squares

4 To make into a patchwork, place two padded squares with right sides together; pin and stitch, following the previous stitching line. Open out flat and continue to join the remaining patches in the same way.

Seminole patchwork

This is one of the quickest and simplest forms of machine-stitched patchwork in which fabric strips of varying width are stitched together, cut into regular strips, rearranged and stitched together again. The resulting patchwork always makes a horizontal band. It is generally used as a decoration, with traditional bright colours contrasted against a plain background.

1 Straighten the end of the first fabric. Then using a ruler and soft pencil or marking pen, mark 1 1/2in (4cm) wide strips across the lengthwise grain and cut out. Cut same size strips from all the fabrics.

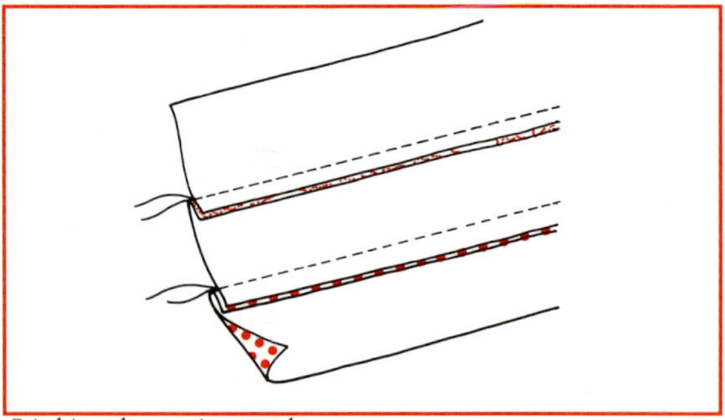

Stitching three strips together

2 Arrange the fabrics in the chosen order. Pin and stitch the strips with right sides together taking 1/4in (5mm) seam allowance. Press the allowances in the same direction and then press the strips well.

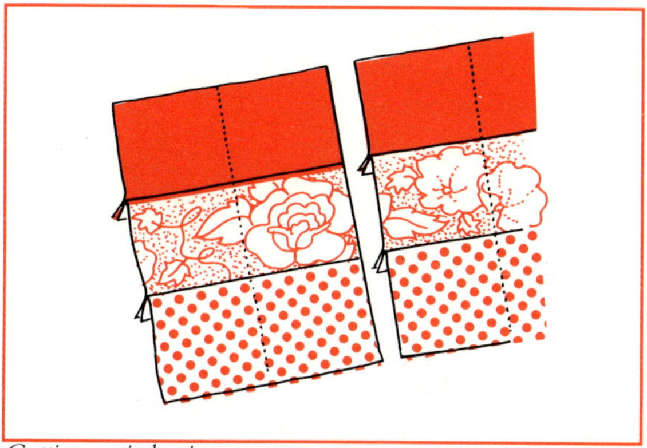

Cutting vertical strips

3 Working from the right side, use a ruler and soft pencil to mark vertical strips each one 1 ½in (4cm) wide and at right angles to the seamlines. Cut out the strips.

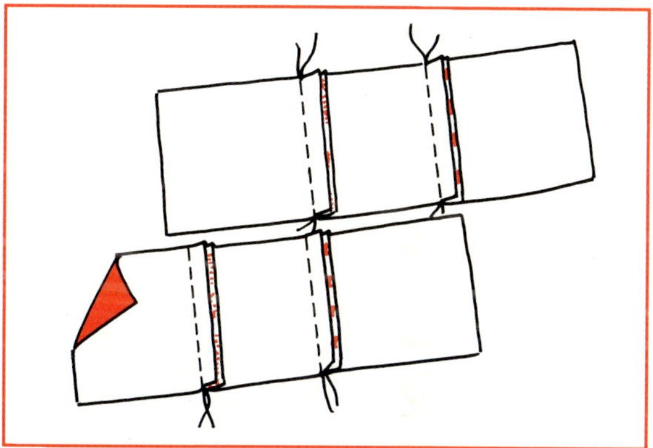

Reassembling the vertical strips

4 These strips can now be rearranged and stitched together again to create diagonal patterns. With right sides facing, take the first two strips and place them together so the right side of the centre square of one strip is level with the left of the centre square on the next strip. Pin and stitch together taking 1/4in (5mm) seam allowance.

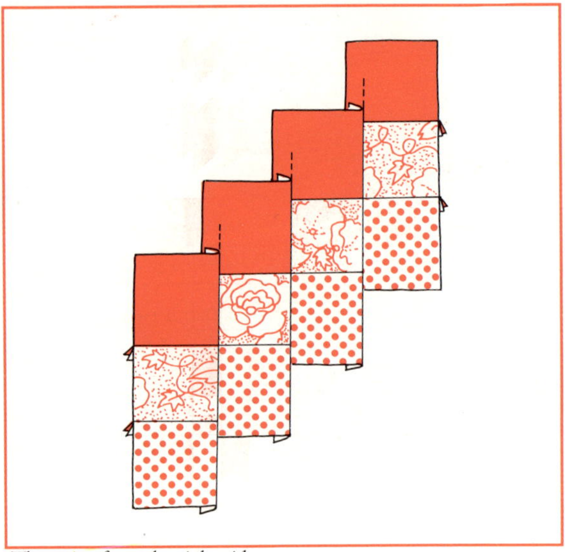

The strips from the right side

5 Continue adding pieces in this way until the desired length. Press the seams to one side.

Forming straight ends to the band

6 To form a horizontal band, mark a vertical line at the lefthand end through the point of the top

Some alternative arrangements

square. Cut to remove a triangle. Stitch this triangle to the righthand end of the piece. Trim off the points along the top and bottom edges, remembering to leave a 1/4in (5mm) seam allowance.

The initial strips do not have to be of equal width and the cutting of the pieced fabric does not have to be in vertical strips as described above. Many more patterns can be formed by cutting pieced strips diagonally and reassembling them into a horizontal band or by turning alternate strips upside down when reforming.

Strip piecing

This is a variation of Seminole patchwork in which the initial piecing of the strips is similar but the resulting fabric is cut in a number of different ways, to be used in traditional block patterns, as shown in the illustrations opposite.

Somerset patchwork

Somerset patchwork, or Folded Star patchwork as it is also called, forms a textured surface with neatly folded layers of fabric triangles held in place with tiny hand stitches. The finished result depends on the accuracy of the cutting and folding of the squares and rectangles of fabric. The use of plain and patterned fabric can change the look of the resulting patterns. The size of the basic squares can vary, but keep them in proportion to the finished piece, tiny squares are used for small items, while larger patches fold up into shapes large enough for cushion covers. The standard size of the basic square should be 2in (5cm) or 3in (7.5cm).

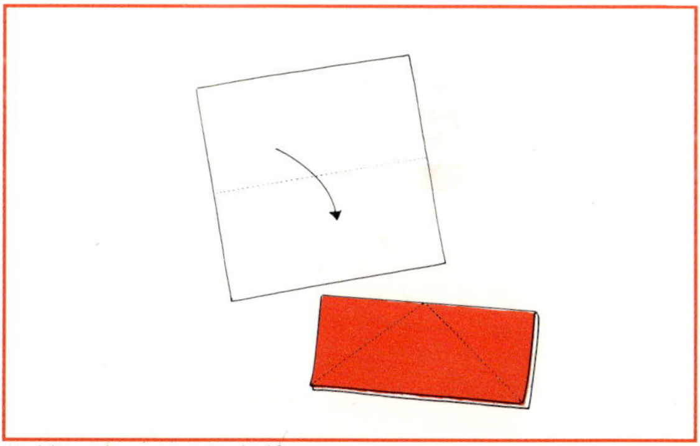

Folding the square in half

1 For each folded triangle, cut a 2 in (5cm) square of fabric on the straight of the grain. Fold the square in half with wrong sides facing.

2 Mark the centre of the base edge. Bring down the top corners to meet together at the centre point forming a triangle. Check that the triangle is even, then press well.

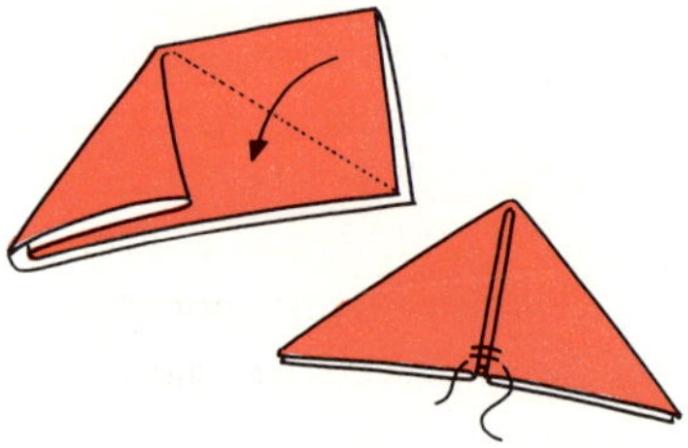

Folding and securing the basic triangle

3 Secure the base edges together with a couple of small backstitches worked using a neutral coloured thread through all thicknesses 1/8in (3mm) up from centre base edge.

4 To form a square pattern, cut a foundation square of fabric. Fold the square diagonally from corner to corner then in half from side to side and from top to base, these form the placement lines. Mark or tack them if necessary.

5 Place the first four triangles on the foundation square with their points meeting together at the centre. Thread a fine needle with a neutral coloured thread and hold the triangles together with a couple

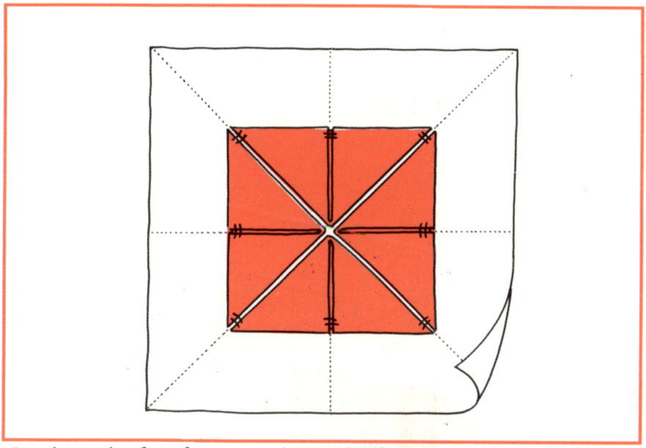

Stitching the first four triangles to the foundation square

of backstitches worked on the spot at the corner of the square and in the centre to hold the triangles together.

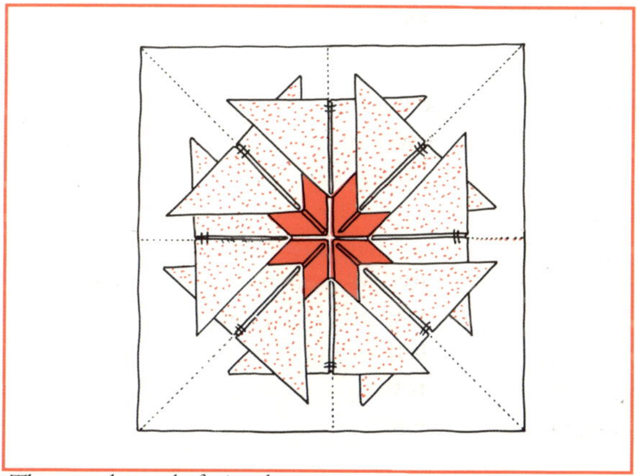

The second round of triangles

6 Place the second round of eight triangles in pairs on the four sides of the centre square, with the points of each triangle the same distance from the central point of the foundation square. Align the central fold of each triangle with the guidelines marked on the foundation square. Stitch each triangle in place in the same way as before.

The third round of triangles

7 In the next round there are sixteen triangles. Place one triangle directly on top of each of the eight in the previous round but with the points at an equal distance apart. Place each of the remaining eight triangles halfway between the others. Stitch in place. Repeat in the same way with each round. The same number of triangles can be used in subsequent rounds to vary the pattern.

8 When the square is complete stitch all around the outer edge.

9 For a circular pattern, form the first round in the same way, then add a second row of eight triangles matching the points along the diagonal marked lines of the foundation square. Keep working around the

A circular placement of the triangles

square, overlapping triangles to form a circular pattern. Check that the spaces between the triangles are the same and the points are equidistant from the centre of the foundation square.

Suffolk puff

Also called "Yo-yo patchwork". The "puffs" which make up this patchwork are gathered up circles of fabric which are caught together in an openwork arrangement. Try creating the patchwork using fine silks and cottons for a delicate result. The gathered-up side of the puffs are the right side. To close the gaps between large puffs, make up smaller versions and stitch them in between the large ones. The puffs can also be sewn together over a coloured or printed background which shows through as a diffused shade.

1 Use a small saucer or an upturned cup as the template for the puffs. Place the template on the wrong side of the fabric and mark around. Remove the template and cut out the circle.

Gathering the circle

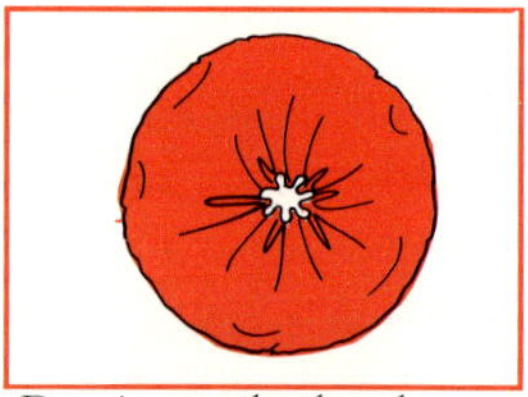
Drawing up the thread

2 Press under 1/8in (3mm) all around each circle. Thread a fine needle with a neutral shade and knot one end. Gather the circle by working running stitches all around the circle through the hem.

3 Pull up the gathering thread to form the puff and fasten off the thread invisibly.

Assembling the puffs

4 To form a patchwork, make up as many puffs as you need. Lay the puffs right side up (the gathered side is the right side) and using a neutral-coloured thread, fasten them together with four small straight stitches worked across adjoining puffs.

FINISHING

Adding a lining

Patchwork needs to be lined to cover and protect the reverse side and to give the finished work body. When the patchwork is to be quilted, wadding is fitted between the patchwork and the lining.

1 Measure the finished patchwork and cut a piece of lining to this size plus 5/8in (1.5cm) seam allowance all around.

2 Lay the patchwork, right side up, on a flat surface. Place the lining on top, right sides together. Smooth out flat and pin together.

Stitching top to lining

Turning right side out

3 Tack and stitch together on three sides and around four corners, leaving an opening centrally in the fourth side. Trim and turn right side out.

4 Turn in the open edges and slipstitch together.

Alternatively, the lining can be fitted to the patchwork top with wrong sides together and pinned. The raw edges can then be bound as described below.

Adding borders

When the patchwork is complete you might decide that it would benefit from a border. Borders have two uses: they frame a design and they increase the size of patchwork which may be necessary to fit a particular bed or cushion form. Borders can either be square cut or mitred at the corners. If a large border is required, it is better to add two or more strips rather than one wide one.

Square cut borders

1 Measure the width of the patchwork across the centre and add twice the seam allowance. Cut two pieces to this measurement for the length and to the chosen width plus twice the seam allowance.

2 Pin and stitch each strip to the top and base edges of the patchwork. Press the border flat.

3 Measure the length of the patchwork including both borders across the centre and add twice the seam allowance. Cut two pieces to this measurement for the length and to the chosen width plus twice the seam allowance.

4 Pin and stitch the side border pieces to the left and right sides of the patchwork. Press flat.

Square cut border

5 Add a lining as described above.

Mitred borders

1 For the top and bottom border strips, measure the width of the patchwork across the centre and add twice the border width and twice the seam allowance. Cut two pieces to this measurement for the length and to the chosen width plus twice the seam allowance. Measure the length in the same way and cut two side border strips.

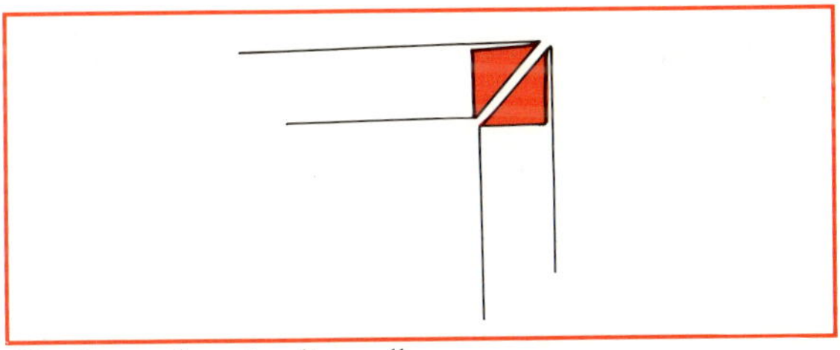

Turning up the strips diagonally

2 Lay the first strip centrally on one of the patchwork sides, right sides together and edges matching.

Turn up one end of the strip diagonally beginning at the edge of the patchwork. Press. Repeat at the ends of each strip to form the diagonal seams.

3 Place the strips together in order, right sides together. Pin and stitch across the diagonal fold lines to within 5/8in (1.5cm) of the inner edge. Trim and press seams open.

Mitred border

4 Place the mitred border to the patchwork top, right sides together. Pin and stitch all around the inner edge of the border. Press the border flat.

5 Add a lining as described above.

Binding the outer edges

There are two ways of finishing the edges of a patchwork with binding.

Straight binding

1 For straight edges, measure the length of the

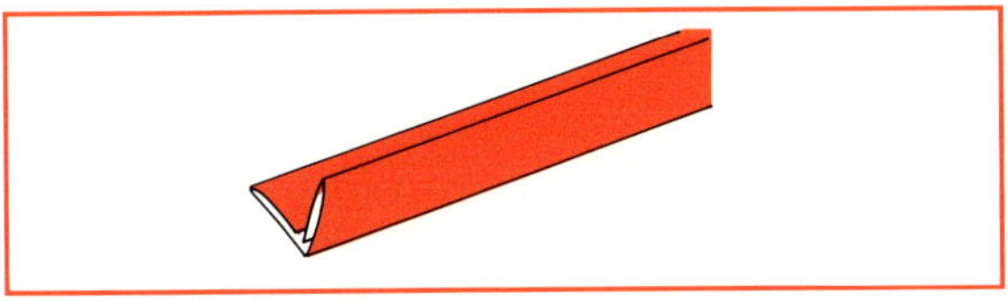

Folding the binding strip

completed patchwork. Mark and cut out two binding strips on the straight of the grain to this length to four times the width of chosen binding. Fold in half lengthwise, then fold the raw edges in to the centre. Press.

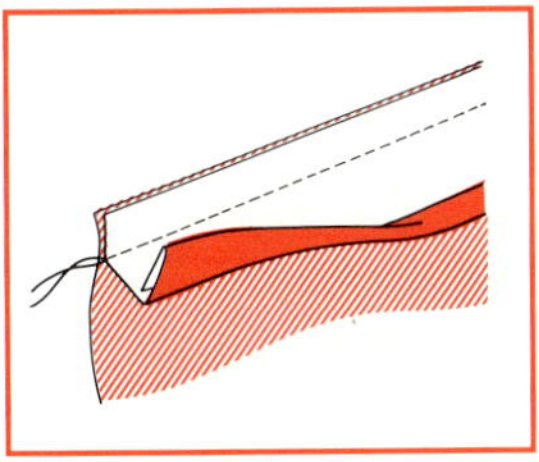

Stitching to right side

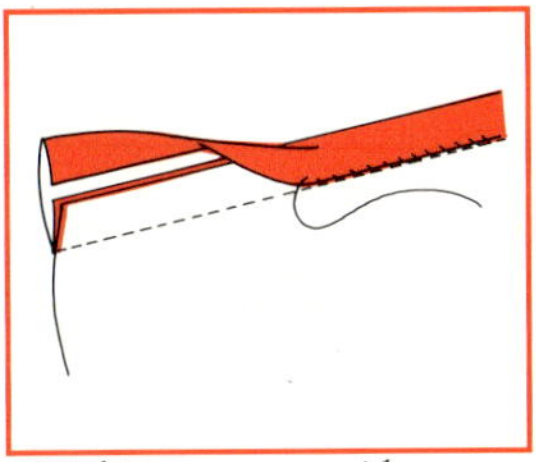

Stitching to wrong side

2 Open out the binding and place on the right side of the patchwork, raw edges matching and right sides together. Pin and stitch down the complete length along the line of the first fold. Turn the binding over the raw edge of the patchwork and to the wrong side, turning under the raw edge of the binding along the pressed fold. Either slipstitch by hand or machine stitch the binding in place in line with the previous stitching. Repeat on the left side.

3 Then bind the top and base edges in the same way, but cutting the binding strips with an extra ½in (1cm) at each end. Centre the binding on the

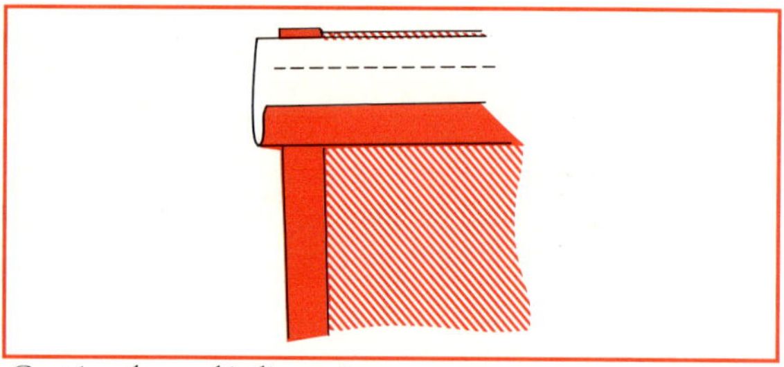

Centring the top binding strip

right side of the patchwork, raw edges matching; pin and stitch in place.

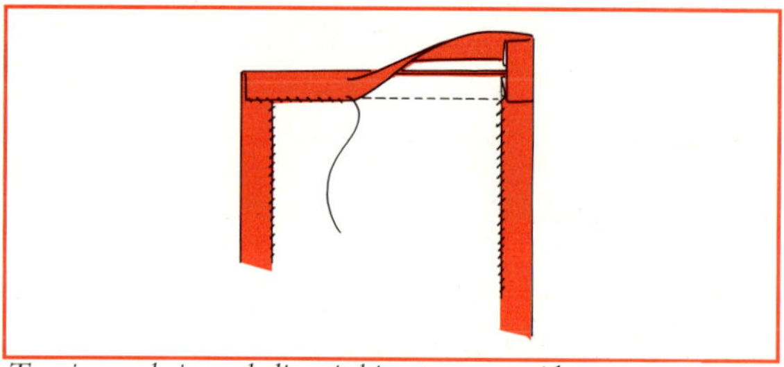

Turning ends in and slip stitching to wrong side

4 Turn the extended ends of the binding over the bound edge, then turn in the binding edge in the usual way and complete the stitching.

Binding with mitred corners

Measure for the length of the binding by adding twice the patchwork length to twice the patchwork width with extra for each mitred corner. For the width measure four times the finished width. Cut a strip on the bias to this length and width, joining if necessary. Fold and press as before.

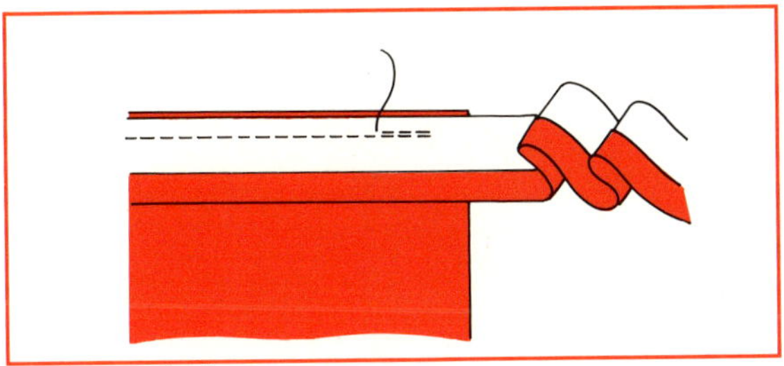

Stitching to the first corner

1 Lay the binding on the right side of the patchwork along the first edge, starting 3in (7.5cm) away from the lefthand corner. Pin and stitch the binding along the edge up to the seam line of the first corner, then work a few stitches in reverse.

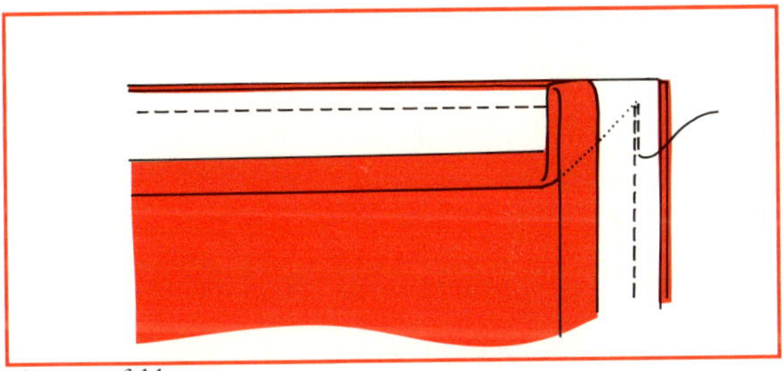

A corner fold

2 Fold the free binding to the right forming a diagonal fold. Place a pin on the inside of this fold, then fold the binding back on itself and along the adjacent edge of the patchwork. Continue stitching the binding along the next side. Repeat at each corner, then join the ends of the binding together to fit, trimming if necessary.

3 Remove the pins at the corners. Press the

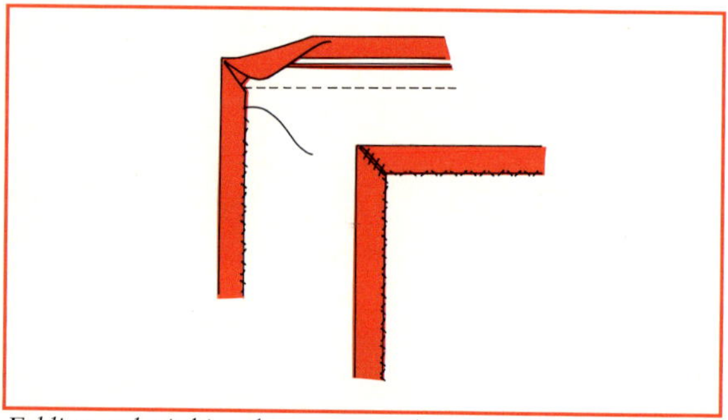

Folding and stitching the corners on the wrong side

binding over the raw edges, forming a mitre at each corner. On the wrong side turn under the raw edge to match previous stitching line. Fold the excess binding under at each corner into a mitre. Finish stitching the edge in place by slipstitching by hand or machine stitching all around the binding.

Part 3:

BLOCKS

The grid system

Most of the traditional block designs are based on a square with an underlying grid. This grid subdivides the square into smaller squares. The grids vary in the number of squares they create and each different grid provides scope for a large number of different designs. The more squares in the grid, the greater the variety of shapes that can be made.

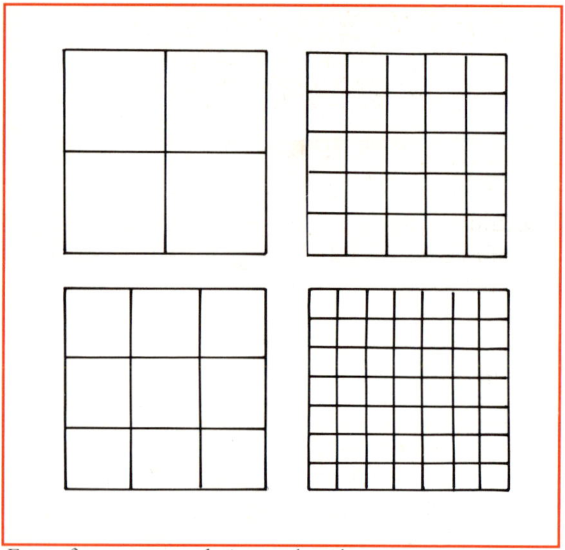

Four-, five-, seven- and nine-patch grids

The squares in the grid are called patches, and designs are grouped together according to which grid they are based on. There are one-patch designs (no grid), four-patch designs (4 squares); five-patch designs (25 squares), seven-patch designs (49 squares) and nine-patch designs (9 squares).

ONE-PATCH DESIGNS

Baby blocks or Tumbling blocks

One of the best-known block patterns made up of diamonds. By using a dark colour on one side of a unit of three diamonds, the building block illusion is created.

Thousand pyramids

A design made up entirely of equilateral triangles, cut from a wide variety of fabrics.

Rail fence

This block is divided into four quarters. In each quarter are four strips of different fabrics. The quarters are placed together in pairs at right angles to each other to form the angular pattern.

Grandmother's garden

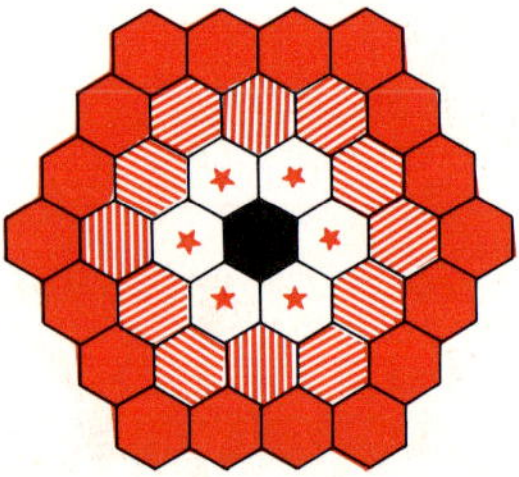

A design made up entirely of hexagons. Each "flower" is created by stitching two rounds of hexagons around a central hexagon. The hexagons in each round are cut from the same fabric. The first round contains six hexagons, the second twelve. The flowers are joined together with a "pathway" which is one hexagon wide. The pathway hexagons are all the same colour.

Four-patch designs

Wild Waves

Each of the four quarters of this design is made up of one large diamond seamed to two smaller diamonds. Using only two colours the result is quite startling.

Kaleidoscope ll

Graduating squares across each quarter with a strip of triangles working diagonally across the quarter.

FIVE-PATCH DESIGNS

Follow the leader

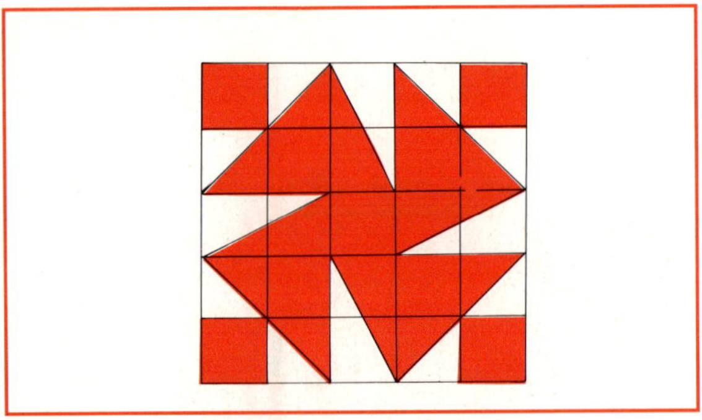

Off-beat triangles are composed of different-sized patches and finished with a square in each corner.

Four & Star

The centre of the block has a square patch in each corner while the outer row of patches are triangles with a square in the centre of each side.

SEVEN-PATCH DESIGNS

Hemstitch

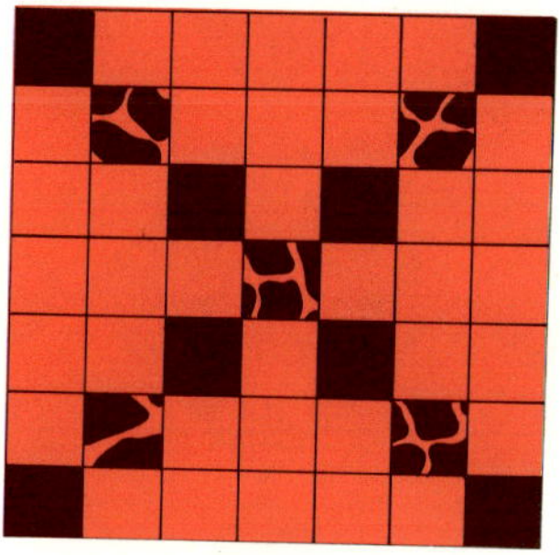

This square shows how a simple arrangement can still create an interesting block.

Hens & chickens

Again a cross of squares bordered by triangles. The centre patch is a contrasting colour.

NINE-PATCH DESIGNS

Rhode island

Made up of triangles and squares this star-shape design is complicated to stitch together.

Birthday cake

A popular design of squares and triangles angled across the block.

Part 4:

CARE AND DISPLAY

Caring for a patchwork

Try to keep patchwork away from direct sunlight as this will weaken the fibres. Not only will the colours fade, but the fabric and sewing threads will begin to rot.

Brush the patchwork regularly to remove dirt and dust.

Always check the fabric content before laundering and dry clean or wash depending on the fabrics. Wash a patchwork piece by hand using a mild detergent in warm water. Do not rub, twist or wring the fabric but gently squeeze out the excess water. Give the patchwork a short spin in a spin dryer and then dry flat. On a fine day, lay a clean sheet on the lawn and lay the patchwork over it to dry. After washing press well.

Storing a patchwork

Textiles need to breathe when they are stored, so do not use plastic. Roll up the patchwork in a clean sheet or with acid-free tissue paper or fold up the patchwork with acid-free tissue paper inside each fold and slip inside a clean pillowcase. If you have folded the patchwork, bring it out once a year and refold it along different lines to prevent the creases from becoming permanent.

After a patchwork has been stored for a while, unroll it and hang it outside on a washing line on a breezy day to air it.

HANGING A PATCHWORK

Although many pieces are made for beds, some are beautiful enough to hang on a wall on permanent display. To do this a fabric casing is attached to the back large enough to take a wooden pole or rod. Make the casing in two sections in case the patchwork needs extra support in the centre.

1 Measure the width of the patchwork top and cut two pieces to half this measurement and 6in (15cm) deep.

2 Form into a tube, turning in and stitching the raw edges at the ends.

3 Flatten the casing and place on the reverse of the patchwork with the top edge just below the binding and leaving a small gap in the centre. Stitch in place by hand with small hemming stitches.

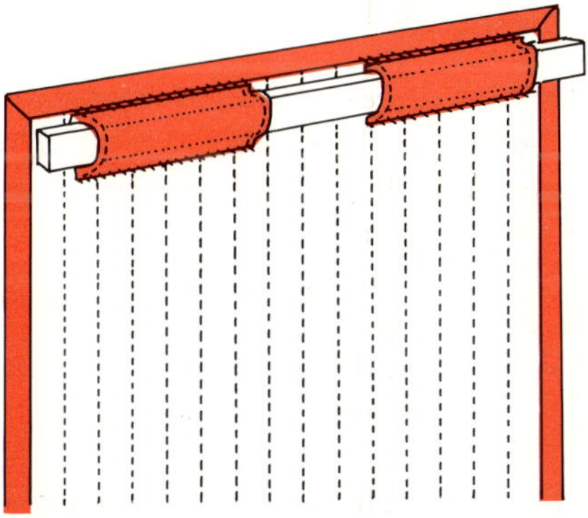

Split fabric casing to take hanging pole

Index